SIDE by SIDE

TEACHER'S GUIDE

Second Edition

3

Steven J. Molinsky
Bill Bliss

Contributing Authors

Mary Ann Perry / John Kopec / with Elizabeth Handley and Katharine Kolodrich

PRENTICE HALL REGENTS   Englewood Cliffs, New Jersey 07632

Editorial/production supervision: Janet Johnston
Art supervision: Karen Salzbach
Manufacturing buyer: Peter Havens
Cover illustration: Richard E. Hill
Cover design: Kenny Beck

Printed in the United States of America

10 9 8 7 6 5 4 3 2

ISBN 0-13-811779-9

Prentice-Hall International (UK) Limited, *London*
Prentice-Hall of Australia Pty. Limited, *Sydney*
Prentice-Hall Canada Inc., *Toronto*
Prentice-Hall Hispanoamericana, S.A., *Mexico*
Prentice-Hall of India Private Limited, *New Delhi*
Prentice-Hall of Japan, Inc., *Tokyo*
Simon & Schuster Asia Pte. Ltd., *Singapore*
Editora Prentice-Hall do Brasil, Ltda., *Rio de Janeiro*

CONTENTS

Side by Side is an English language program for young-adult and adult learners from beginning to high-intermediate levels. The program consists of Student Books 1, 2, 3, 4 and accompanying Activity Workbooks, Teacher's Guides, an Audio Program, a Picture Program, and a Testing Program.

Side by Side offers students a dynamic, communicative approach to the language. Through the methodology of Guided Conversations, *Side by Side* engages students in meaningful conversational exchanges within carefully structured grammatical frameworks, and then encourages students to break away from the textbook and *use* these frameworks to create conversations *on their own*. All the language practice that is generated through the texts results in active communication taking place between students...practicing speaking together, "side by side."

The texts provide all-skills language practice through reading, writing, and listening activities that are totally integrated with the conversational exercises. Short reading selections offer enjoyable reading practice that simultaneously reinforces the grammatical focus of each chapter. *Check-Up* activities provide focused practice in reading comprehension and vocabulary development. *Listening* exercises enable students to develop their aural comprehension skills through a variety of listening activities. And *In Your Own Words* activities provide topics and themes for student compositions and classroom discussions in which students rite about their friends, families, homes, schools, and themselves.

The goal of *Side by Side* is to engage students in active, meaningful communicative practice with the language. The aim of the *Side by Side Teacher's Guides* is to offer guidelines and strategies to help achieve that goal.

STUDENT TEXT OVERVIEW

Chapter Opening Pages

The opening page of each chapter provides an overview of the new grammatical structures treated in the chapter.

Conversation Lessons

1. GRAMMATICAL PARADIGMS

A new grammatical structure appears first in the form of a grammatical paradigm, or "grammar box"—a simple schema of the structure. (Grammar boxes are in a light blue tint.) These paradigms are meant to be a reference point for students as they proceed through a lesson's conversational activities. While these paradigms highlight the structures being taught, they are not intended to be goals in themselves. Students are not expected to memorize or parrot back these rules. Rather, we want students to take part in conversations that show they can *use* these rules correctly.

2. MODEL GUIDED CONVERSATIONS

Model Guided Conversations serve as the vehicles for introducing new grammatical structures, as well as many communicative uses of English. Since the model becomes the basis for all of the exercises that follow, it is essential that students be given sufficient practice with it before proceeding with the lesson.

3. SIDE BY SIDE EXERCISES

In the numbered exercises that follow the model, students pair up and work "side by side," placing new content into the given conversational framework. These exercises form the core learning activity of each conversation lesson.

Reading Lessons

1. READING SELECTIONS

Short reading selections offer enjoyable reading practice that simultaneously reinforces the grammatical focus of each chapter. Accompanying illustrations serve as visual cues that guide learners through the reading and help to clarify both context and new vocabulary.

2. CHECK-UP

Check-Up exercises provide focused practice in reading comprehension and vocabulary development. Also, listening exercises enable students to develop their aural comprehension skills through a variety of listening activities.

3. IN YOUR OWN WORDS

These activities provide topics and themes for student compositions and classroom discussions. Students write about their friends, families, homes, schools, jobs, and themselves.

On Your Own and *How About You?* Activities

These student-centered activities give students valuable opportunities to apply lesson content to their own lives and experiences and to share opinions in class. Through these activities, students bring to the classroom new content, based on their interests, their backgrounds, and their imaginations. Activities include role plays, questions about the students' real world, and topics for discussion and debate.

Summary Pages

Summary pages at the end of each chapter highlight functional language and grammatical structures covered in that chapter. They are useful as a review and study guide after students have completed the chapter.

ANCILLARY MATERIALS

Activity Workbooks

The Activity Workbooks offer a variety of exercises for reinforcement, fully coordinated with the student texts. A special feature of the Activity Workbooks is the inclusion of rhythm, stress, pronunciation, and intonation exercises. Periodic check-up tests are also included.

Audio Program

The Student Text tapes are especially designed to serve as a student's speaking partner, making conversation practice possible even when the student is studying alone. In addition to the guided conversation exercises, the tapes contain the listening comprehension exercises along with recordings of all of the reading selections in the text.

The Activity Workbook tapes contain the listening, pronunciation, rhythm, stress, and intonation exercises in the workbooks.

Picture Program

Side by Side Picture Cards illustrate key concepts and vocabulary items. They can be used for introduction of new material, for review, for enrichment, and for role-playing activities. Suggestions for their use are included in the Teacher's Guide. Also, the Appendix to the Teacher's Guide contains a triple listing of the Picture Cards: numerically, alphabetically, and by category.

Testing Program

The *Side by Side* Testing Program offers a placement test as well as mid-term and final examinations for each level of the program.

FORMAT OF THE TEACHER'S GUIDE

Chapter Overview

The Chapter Overview provides the following:

- Functional and grammatical highlights of the chapter
- A listing of new vocabulary and expressions
- Language and culture notes that apply to the chapter as a whole

Step-by-Step Lesson Guide

Included for each conversation lesson are the following:

- FOCUS of the lesson
- GETTING READY: suggestions for introducing the new concepts in the lesson
- INTRODUCING THE MODEL: steps for introducing the model conversation
- SIDE BY SIDE EXERCISES: suggestions for practicing the exercises, as well as a listing of new vocabulary
- LANGUAGE AND CULTURE NOTES
- WORKBOOK: page references for exercises in the Activity Workbook that correspond to the particular lesson
- EXPANSION ACTIVITIES: optional activities for review and reinforcement of the content of the lesson

Included for each reading lesson are the following:

- FOCUS of the lesson
- NEW VOCABULARY contained in the reading
- PREVIEWING THE STORY: an optional preliminary stage before students begin to read the selection
- READING THE STORY: suggestions for presenting the story as well as questions to check students' comprehension
- CHECK-UP: answer keys and listening scripts for check-up exercises
- IN YOUR OWN WORDS: suggestions for doing these writing and discussion exercises

Workbook Answer Key and Listening Scripts

Answers and listening scripts for all exercises contained in the Activity Workbooks are provided at the end of each chapter of the Teacher's Guide.

GENERAL TEACHING STRATEGIES

Introducing the Model

Since the model conversation forms the basis of each lesson, it is essential that students practice the model several times in a variety of ways before going on to the exercises. The following eight steps are recommended for introducing a model conversation. Of course, you should feel free to modify them to suit your own particular teaching style and the needs of your students.

1. Have students look at the model illustration. This helps establish the context of the conversation.
2. *Set the scene.* For every model, one or two lines are suggested in this Teacher's Guide for you to use to "set the scene" of the dialog for your students.
3. *Present the model.* With books closed, have students listen as you present the model or play the tape one or more times. To make the presentation of the model as realistic as possible, you might draw two stick figures on the board to represent the speakers in the dialog. You can also show that two people are speaking by changing your position or by shifting your weight from one foot to the other as you say each speaker's lines.
4. *Full-Class Choral Repetition.* Model each line and have the whole class repeat in unison.

5. Have students open their books and look at the dialog. Ask if there are any questions, and check understanding of new vocabulary. (All new vocabulary in the model is listed here. The illustration and the context of the dialog normally help to clarify the meaning of new words.)

6. *Group Choral Repetition.* Divide the class in half. Model line A and have Group 1 repeat; model line B and have Group 2 repeat. Continue this with all the lines of the model.

7. *Choral Conversation.* Groups 1 and 2 practice the dialog twice, without teacher model. First Group 1 is Speaker A and Group 2 is Speaker B; then reverse.

8. Call on one or two pairs of students to present the dialog.

In steps 6, 7, and 8 you should encourage students to look up from their books and *say* the lines rather than read them. (Students can of course refer to their books when necessary.) *The goal here is not memorization or complete mastery of the model.* Rather, students should become familiar with the model and feel comfortable saying it.

At this point, if you feel that additional practice is necessary before going on to the exercises, you can do Choral Conversation in small groups or by rows.

Side by Side Exercises

The numbered exercises that follow the model form the core learning activity in each conversation lesson. Here students use the pictures and word cues to create conversations based on the structure of the model. Since all language practice in these lessons is conversational, you will always call on a pair of students to do each exercise. *Your* primary role is to serve as a resource to the class: to help with the structures, new vocabulary, intonation, and pronunciation.

The following three steps are recommended in each lesson for practicing the *Side by Side* exercises. (Students should be given thorough practice with the first two exercises before going on.)

1. Exercise 1: Introduce any new vocabulary in the exercise. Call on two students to present the dialog. Then do Choral Repetition and Choral Conversation Practice.

2. Exercise 2: Same as for Exercise 1.

3. For the remaining exercises, there are two options: either Full-Class Practice or Pair Practice.

   Full-Class Practice: Call on a pair of students to do each exercise. Introduce new vocabulary one exercise at a time. (For more practice, call on other pairs of students, or do Choral Repetition or Choral Conversation.)

   Pair Practice: Introduce new vocabulary for all the exercises. Next have students practice all the exercises in pairs. Then have pairs present the exercises to the class. (For more practice, do Choral Repetition or Choral Conversation.)

   The choice of Full-Class Practice or Pair Practice should be determined by the content of the particular lesson, the size and composition of the class, and your own teaching style. You might also wish to vary your approach from lesson to lesson.

Suggestions for Pairing Up Students: Whether you use Full-Class Practice or Pair Practice, you can select students for the pairs in various ways. You might want to pair students by ability, since students of similar ability might work more efficiently together than students of dissimilar ability. On the other hand, you might wish to pair a weaker student with a stronger one. The slower student benefits from this pairing, while the more advanced student strengthens his or her abilities by helping the partner.

You should also encourage students to *look at* each other when speaking. This makes the conversational nature of the language practice more realistic. One way of ensuring this is *not* to call on two students who are sitting next to each other. Rather, call on students in different parts of the room and encourage them to look at each other when saying their lines.

Presenting New Vocabulary

Many new vocabulary words are introduced in each conversation lesson. The illustration normally helps to convey the meaning, and the new words are written for students to see and use in these conversations. In addition, you might:

1. write the new word on the board or on a word card,
2. say the new word several times and ask students to repeat chorally and individually, and

3. help clarify the meaning with *Side by Side* Picture Cards or your own visuals (pictures from magazines, newspapers, or your own drawings).

Students might also find it useful to keep a notebook in which they write each new word, its meaning, and a sentence using that word.

Open-Ended Exercises (the "Blank Box")

In many lessons, the final exercise is an open-ended one. This is indicated in the text by a blank box. Here the students are expected to create conversations based on the structure of the model, but with vocabulary that they select themselves. This provides students with an opportunity for creativity, while still focusing on the particular structure being practiced. These open-ended exercises can be done orally in class and/or assigned as homework for presentation in class the next day. Encourage students to use dictionaries to find new words they want to use.

On Your Own

On Your Own activities offer students the opportunity to contribute content of their own within the grammatical framework of the lesson. You should introduce these activities in class and assign them as homework for presentation in class the next day. In this way, students will automatically review the previous day's grammar while contributing new and inventive content of their own.

These activities are meant for simultaneous grammar reinforcement and vocabulary building. Students should be encouraged to use a dictionary when completing the *On Your Own* activities. In this way, they will not only use the words they know, but the words they would *like* to know in order to really bring their interests, backgrounds, and imaginations into the classroom.

As a result, students will teach each other new vocabulary and also share a bit of their lives with others in the class.

How About You?

How About You? activities are intended to provide students with additional opportunities to tell about themselves. Have students do these activities in pairs or as a class.

Expansion Activities

For each conversation lesson, the Teacher's Guide contains ideas for optional review and reinforcement activities. Feel free to pick and choose or vary the activities to fit the particular needs and learning styles of students in your class. The ideas are meant to serve as a springboard for developing your own learning activities.

General Guiding Principles for Working with Guided Conversations

1. When doing the exercises, students should practice *speaking* to each other, rather than *reading* to each other. Therefore, while students will need to refer to the text to be able to practice the conversations, they should not read the lines word by word. Rather, they should practice scanning a full line and then look up from the book and *speak* the line to another person.

2. Throughout, teachers should use the book to teach proper intonation and gesture. (Capitalized words are used to indicate spoken emphasis.) Students should be encouraged to truly *act out* the dialogs in a strong and confident voice.

3. Use of the texts should be as *student-centered* as possible. Modeling by the teacher should be efficient and economical, but students should have every opportunity to model for each other when they are capable of doing so.

4. Vocabulary can and should be effectively taught in the context of the conversation being practiced. Very often it will be possible to grasp the meaning from the conversation or its accompanying illustration. Teachers should spend time drilling vocabulary in isolation *only* if they feel it is absolutely essential.

5. Students need not formally study or be able to produce grammatical rules. The purpose of the texts is to engage students in active communicative practice that gets them to *use* the language according to these rules.

6. Students should be given every opportunity to apply their own lives and creative contributions to the exercises. This is directly provided for in the blank boxes at the end of many lessons as well as in the *On Your Own* and *How About You?* activities, but teachers can look to *all* exercises with an eye toward expanding them to the real world of the classroom or to the students' real lives.

Introducing Reading Selections

You may wish to preview each story either by briefly setting the scene or by having students talk about the illustrations or predict the content of the story from the title. You may also find it useful to introduce new vocabulary items before they are encountered in the story. On the other hand, you may prefer to skip the previewing step and instead have students experience the subject matter and any unfamiliar words in the context of the initial reading of the story.

There are many ways in which students can read and talk about the stories. Students may read silently to themselves or follow along as the story is read by you, by one or more students, or on the tape. You should then ask students if they have any questions and check understanding of new vocabulary. For each reading selection, the Teacher's Guide provides a list of questions based on the story. You may wish to check students' comprehension by asking these questions before going on to the Check-Up exercises.

Q & A Exercises

Q & A exercises are included as part of the Check-Up after many of the reading selections. These exercises are designed to give students conversation practice based on information contained in the stories. Italic type in the Q & A model highlights the words to be replaced by different information contained in the reading.

Call on a pair of students to present the Q & A model. Have students work in pairs to create new dialogs based on the model, and then call on pairs to present their new dialogs to the class.

In Your Own Words

These activities are designed to guide students in their creation of original stories. Students are asked to write about topics such as their homes, schools, friends, families, and themselves.

You should go over the instructions for the activities and make sure students understand what is expected. Students should do the activity as written homework, using a dictionary for any new words they wish to use. Then have students present and discuss what they have written, in pairs or as a class.

Activity Workbooks

The exercises in the Activity Workbooks are fully coordinated with the student texts. For each conversation lesson in the student text, the Teacher's Guide indicates which particular workbook exercises provide supplementary practice. This cross-referencing information can also be found at the back of the workbooks.

The workbooks provide intensive practice in grammar reinforcement, reading, writing, listening, and pronunciation. A special feature is the inclusion of exercises in rhythm, stress, and intonation of English. In these exercises, black dots are used as a kind of musical notation system to indicate the number of "beats" on each line. The dots also serve to indicate the primary word stresses and graphically show the reduced emphasis on the surrounding, unstressed words. Have students first listen to these exercises on tape, and then practice saying them. For each exercise, establish the rhythm for the students by clapping, tapping, or finger-snapping on each "beat," as indicated by the black dots. Students also enjoy doing this as they perform these exercises.

In conclusion, we have attempted to make the study of English a lively and relevant experience for our students. While we hope that we have conveyed to you the substance of our textbooks, we also hope that we have conveyed the spirit: that learning the language can be interactive...student-centered...and fun.

Steven J. Molinsky
Bill Bliss

GRAMMAR

Present Continuous Tense

(I am)	I'm	
(He is) (She is) (It is)	He's She's It's	eating.
(We are) (You are) (They are)	We're You're They're	

Am	I	
Is	he she it	eating?
Are	we you they	

To Be: Short Answers

	I	am.
Yes,	he she it	is.
	we you they	are.

	I'm	not.
No,	he she it	isn't.
	we you they	aren't.

Simple Present Tense

I We You They	eat.
He She It	eats.

Do	I we you they	eat?
Does	he she it	

Yes,	I we you they	do.
	he she it	does.

No,	I we you they	don't.
	he she it	doesn't.

Subject Pronouns	Possessive Adjectives	Object Pronouns
I	my	me
he	his	him
she	her	her
it	its	it
we	our	us
you	your	you
they	their	them

FUNCTIONS

Asking for and Reporting Information

Are you busy?
  Yes, I am. I'm *studying*.
What are you *studying*?
  I'm *studying English*.

Who are you calling?

What are you doing?
  I'm *practicing the piano*.

What *are George and Herman* talking about?

What *are you* complaining about?

What's *your teacher's* name?
What are their names?

What do you do?

When do you *go to class*?

Where are you from?
Where do you live now?
Where do you *work*?

How old *are they*?

How often do you *watch TV*?

Do you *practice* very often?
  Yes, I do.

Is *he* a good *football player*?
  Yes, *he* is.

Are you married?
Are you single?

Do you live with *your parents*?
Do you live *alone*?

His football coach says *he's excellent*.
His friends tell *him he plays football better than anyone else*.

Inquiring about Likes/Dislikes

Do you like to *ski*?

What do you like to do *in your free time*?

Expressing Inability

I'm not a very good *skier*.

NEW VOCABULARY

aerobics	cook (n)	music teacher	tennis coach
argue	dance ballet (v)	once	twice
army	dance teacher	portrait	typist
ballet dancer	electric bill	professional (adj)	whenever
Beethoven	football coach	Shakespeare	Whistler
bill	free time	skater	
coach (n)	interests	stay after	once a *day*
compose	Little Red Riding Hood	swimmer	twice a *day*

LANGUAGE NOTES

1. **Simple Present Tense**

   a. In this chapter, the simple present tense is used to express

   habitual activity: *How often do you call him?*
   I call him every Sunday.

   and factual statements: *I live in Tokyo.*
   I have three children.

   b. This tense may also be used to express scheduled events in the future:
   The bus comes at ten o'clock tonight.

   c. Adverbs of frequency, such as *always, sometimes, never,* and frequency time expressions, such as *every week, once a month,* are commonly used with the simple present tense.

2. **Present Continuous Tense**

   a. In this chapter, the present continuous tense is used to express events that are happening right now:
   What are you doing?   *What's Jane knitting?*
   I'm practicing the piano.   *She's knitting a sweater.*

   b. This tense may also be used to express temporary activities or events:
   We're washing the dishes in the bathtub because the sink is broken.
   Barbara isn't feeling very well today.

   and future events that differ from the expected routine:
   I'm getting married tomorrow.
   We're moving to New York next month.

   c. Certain verbs, when used as *stative verbs,* are not used in the present continuous tense. These verbs include *think, know, want, need, see, hear, seem, like, love.*

   I think you're right.   *We need some more paper.*   *She seems sad.*
   I don't know them.   *I can't see you.*   *Bill doesn't like milk.*
   They want some tea.   *She didn't hear that.*   *I love you.*

3. **Pronunciation Problems**

   a. Some students have difficulty pronouncing the final *s* in the 3rd person singular forms of the simple present tense. For example: *He studies, She swims.*

   b. Similarly, some students have trouble pronouncing the final *s* in the contractions *he's, she's,* and *it's.*

   The dictations suggested in the Expansion Activities and the Workbook exercises will help students focus on these sounds.

Text Page 2: *They're Busy*

FOCUS

Review of the present continuous tense

GETTING READY

1. Review the present continuous tense.

   a. Form sentences with the words in the left-hand box at the top of the page. Have students repeat chorally. For example:

      "I'm eating."
      "He's eating."

      Check students' pronunciation of the final *s* sound in *He's, She's, It's.*

   b. Use *Side by Side* Picture Cards for verbs or your own visuals.

      Ask students "What _____ doing?" and have students answer individually, then chorally. For example:

A. What's he doing?	A. What's she doing?	A. What are they doing?
B. He's cooking.	B. She's reading.	B. They're studying.

   c. Have students role play people in the visuals. Ask students "What are you doing?" For example:

A. What are you doing?	A. What are you and (Jim) doing?
B. I'm cooking.	B. We're cooking.

2. Review *Yes/No* questions and affirmative short answers. Form sentences with the words in the 2nd and 3rd boxes at the top of the page. Have students repeat chorally. For example:

"Am I eating?"	"Is he eating?"
"Yes, I am."	"Yes, he is."

3. Use *Side by Side* Picture Cards or your own visuals to practice short answers.

   a. Point to each visual and ask "Is _____ _____ing?" Have students respond with the affirmative short answer. For example:

A. Is she eating?	A. Are they playing baseball?
B. Yes, she is.	B. Yes, they are.

   b. Point to each visual and call on pairs of students to ask and answer as above.

INTRODUCING THE MODEL

1. Have students look at the model illustration.
2. Set the scene: "A girl is talking to her father."
3. With books closed, have students listen as you present the model or play the tape one or more times.
4. **Full-Class Choral Repetition:** Model each line and have students repeat.
5. Have students open their books and look at the dialog. Ask students if they have any questions; check understanding of vocabulary.

6. **Group Choral Repetition:** Divide the class in half. Model line A and have Group 1 repeat; model line B and have Group 2 repeat, and so on.

7. **Choral Conversation:** Groups 1 and 2 practice the dialog twice, without teacher model. First, Group 1 is Speaker A and Group 2 is Speaker B; then reverse.

8. Call on one or two pairs of students to present the dialog.

   (For additional practice, do Choral Conversation in small groups or by rows.)

SIDE BY SIDE EXERCISES

Examples

---

1. A. Is Helen busy?
   B. Yes, she is. She's cooking.
   A. What's she cooking?
   B. She's cooking spaghetti.

2. A. Is Tom busy?
   B. Yes, he is. He's reading.
   A. What's he reading?
   B. He's reading the newspaper.

---

1. **Exercise 1:** Call on two students to present the dialog. Then do Choral Repetition and Choral Conversation Practice.

2. **Exercise 2:** Same as above.

3. **Exercises 3–9:**

New vocabulary: 8. *compose*   9. *portrait*

Culture Notes

Exercise 8: Ludwig von Beethoven (1770–1827) was a German composer of classical music.

Exercise 9: James McNeill Whistler (1834–1903) was a U.S. painter who is best-known for a painting of his mother in a rocking chair.

Either

Full-Class Practice: Introduce the new vocabulary before doing Exercises 8 and 9. Call on a pair of students to do each exercise. (For more practice, call on other pairs of students, or do Choral Repetition or Choral Conversation.)

or

Pair Practice: Introduce all the new vocabulary. Next have students practice all the exercises in pairs. Then have pairs present the exercises to the class. (For more practice, do Choral Repetition or Choral Conversation.)

WORKBOOK

Pages 1–3

Exercise Note

Workbook p. 2: For additional oral practice with Exercise B, have students act out the conversations.

EXPANSION ACTIVITIES

1. **Review Verbs with Visuals**

   Use *Side by Side* Picture Cards for verbs and community locations or your own visuals to review the present continuous tense.

   Hold up each visual and call on students to ask and answer as many questions as possible about what the person or people in the visual are doing. For example:

   (*Side by Side* Picture Card 36)   A. What's she doing?
   B. She's cleaning her apartment.

   (*Side by Side* Picture Card 220)   A. What's he doing?
   B. He's playing the piano.
   A. What are the other people doing?
   B. They're listening to the concert/music.

2. **Role Play: *A Telephone Conversation***

   a. Write this conversational model on the board:

   A. Hi, _____. This is _____. Would you like to come over and visit?
   B. I'm really sorry, but I can't. I'm _____ing right now.
   A. Oh, well. Maybe some other time.
   B. Sure. Thanks for calling.

   ---

   b. Call on pairs of students to role play the telephone conversation, using any vocabulary they wish. For example:

   A. Hi, Tom. This is Paul. Would you like to come over and visit?
   B. I'm really sorry, but I can't. I'm studying right now.
   A. Oh, well. Maybe some other time.
   B. Sure. Thanks for calling.

3. **Dictation**

   Dictate the following sentences to your students. Read each sentence twice.

   1. She's typing a letter.
   2. What's he doing?
   3. He's knitting a sweater.
   4. They're studying.
   5. We're reading the newspaper.
   6. I'm baking cookies.
   7. Are you cooking?
   8. What's he cleaning?
   9. What are they painting?

4. **Pantomime: *Guess What I'm Doing?***

   a. Write the names of activities on cards and give one to each student in the class. Sample activities are:

bake a pie	type a letter	paint a portrait	knit a sweater	use a computer
wait for the bus	start a car	ride a bicycle	do homework	count money

b. Have some students pantomime the activities on their cards and others guess what they're doing:

    A. Are you _____ing?
    B. Yes, I am./No, I'm not.

Variant: Pantomime Game

a. Divide the class into teams.

b. One member of the team pantomimes an activity, and the other teams take turns guessing.

c. A team scores one point for each activity it guesses. The team with the most points wins the game.

Text Page 3: *What Are They Doing?*

FOCUS

> • Contrast of the simple present and present continuous tenses
> • Review of question formation

GETTING READY

1. Review the simple present tense by talking about habitual activities.

    a. Write the adverbs below on the board. Review the pronunciation. Say each word and have students repeat chorally: *always, often, sometimes, rarely, never.*

    b. Make a statement about yourself, such as:

    > "I always study English on the weekend."
    > "I never worry about things."
    > "I sometimes drive too fast."
    > "I usually sing in the shower."
    > "I never dance at parties."

    After each statement, ask students "How about you?" Have students respond with statements about themselves. For example:

    > Teacher: I always study English on the weekend. How about you?
    > Student A: I rarely study English on the weekend.
    > Student B: I usually study English on the weekend.

2. Review *he, she,* and *they* forms in the simple present tense.

    a. Put these cues on the board:

		work	*study*	*like to eat in restaurants*	*do exercises*
	Tom	bank	math	Italian	morning
	Jane	museum	French	French	night

    b. Set the scene: "Tom and Jane are happily married. They like each other very much, but they're very different." Then tell the story:

    1. Both Tom and Jane work.
        Tom works in a bank.
        Jane works in a museum.

    2. They both study in the evening.
        Tom studies math.
        Jane studies French.

    3. They both like to eat in restaurants.
        Tom likes to eat in Italian restaurants.
        Jane likes to eat in French restaurants.

    4. They both do exercises every day.
        Tom does his exercises in the morning.
        Jane does her exercises at night.

    c. Put the following guide on the board and call on pairs of students to create conversations about Tom and Jane.

```
A.  Do   ⎫ _____ ?
    Does ⎭
B.  Yes, _____ .
    _____ .
```

For example:

    A. Do Tom and Jane work?
    B. Yes, they do.
        Tom works in a bank, and Jane works in a museum.

    A. Does Jane study in the evening?
    B. Yes, she does.
        She studies French.

INTRODUCING THE MODEL

1. Have students look at the model illustration.
2. Set the scene: "Two people are talking."
3. Present the model.
4. Full-Class Choral Repetition.
5. Ask students if they have any questions; check understanding of new vocabulary: *whenever.*
6. Group Choral Repetition.
7. Choral Conversation.
8. Call on one or two pairs of students to present the dialog.
    (For additional practice, do Choral Conversation in small groups or by rows.)

SIDE BY SIDE EXERCISES

Examples

```
1.  A.  What's Edward doing?
    B.  He's baking bread.
    A.  Does he bake bread very often?
    B.  Yes, he does. He bakes bread whenever he can.

2.  A.  What's Janet doing?
    B.  She's swimming.
    A.  Does she swim very often?
    B.  Yes, she does. She swims whenever she can.
```

1. **Exercise 1:** Call on two students to present the dialog. Then do Choral Repetition and Choral Conversation Practice.
2. **Exercise 2:** Same as above.
3. **Exercises 3–8:**

```
New vocabulary:   8.  do aerobics
```

Culture Note

Exercise 4: William Shakespeare (1564–1616) was a famous English author. His plays have become well-known classics to students of English literature all over the world.

Either Full-Class Practice or Pair Practice.

4. **Exercise 9:** Have students use the model as a guide to create their own conversations, using vocabulary of their choice. (They can use any names and activities they wish.) Encourage students to use dictionaries to find new words they want to use. This exercise can be done orally in class or for written homework. If you assign it for homework, you should do one example in class to make sure students understand what's expected. Have students present their conversations in class the next day.

WORKBOOK

Pages 4–5

Exercise Note

Workbook p. 4: Students use any vocabulary they wish to complete the sentences. Have students compare their answers.

EXPANSION ACTIVITIES

1. Listening and Pronunciation Practice

a. Put on the board:

b. Have students listen as you read each of the following sentences with blanks. Have students choose the correct pronoun on the board, say it, and then repeat the entire sentence chorally and individually.

1. _____ goes to school every day.
2. _____ play baseball every weekend.
3. _____ practice the piano often.
4. _____ read Shakespeare at night.
5. _____ always studies English.
6. _____ always go to movies after work.
7. _____ never drive carefully.
8. _____ usually speaks very slowly.
9. _____ usually take the bus to school.
10. _____ always cleans the apartment.

Example:

You: _____ goes to school every day.
Students: He: He goes to school every day.

2. Pronunciation Practice

Write pairs of verbs on the board with and without the final *s*. Have students practice saying these words chorally and individually. For example:

go–goes	read–reads	play–plays	bake–bakes
cook–cooks	study–studies	swim–swims	write–writes

3. Role Play Using Visuals: Verb Contrast

a. Write this conversational model on the board:

> A.   What _____ doing?
> B.   _____ing.
> A.   That's strange! _____ never _____!
> B.   Well, _____ing today!

Use *Side by Side* Picture Cards for verbs, your own visuals, or word cues on the board. If you use word cues, include a name and a verb. For example:

> Mary
> swim

> Peter
> exercise

b. Point to a visual or word cue and call on a pair of students to create a conversation based on the model. For example:

> *(Side by Side* Picture Card 126: *skate)*
>
> A.   What are they doing?
> B.   They're skating.
> A.   That's strange! They never skate!
> B.   Well, they're skating today!

4. Tell More about Situation 6

Have students look at the illustration for Exercise 6. Ask students the questions below. These questions allow students to use their imaginations to tell more about Mary.

> What's Mary doing?
> Does she write to her grandparents very often?
> What does she write to them about?
> Does she see them very often?
> What does Mary do with her grandparents when she sees them?

5. What Do You Think They're Doing Now?

a. Write the names of some famous people on the board. For example:

> the President   Elizabeth Taylor*
> the Queen   Eddie Murphy
> the Prime Minister
>
> *or any other currently popular entertainment stars

b. Ask about these famous people. For example:

> Teacher: It's midnight in Washington, D.C.
>   What's the President doing?
>
> Student 1: He's sleeping.
> Student 2: He's probably talking on the *hot line.*
> Student 3: I think he's meeting with the Secretary of State.

Teacher:	It's 4 P.M. in London.
	What's the Queen doing?

Student 1:	She's probably having tea.
Student 2:	She's working at her office.
Student 3:	Maybe she's playing with her grandchildren.

Teacher:	It's 10 A.M. in Hollywood.
	What's Elizabeth Taylor doing?

Student 1:	She's swimming in her pool.
Student 2:	She's probably acting in a movie.
Student 3:	I'm sure she's still sleeping.

Encourage students to be imaginative when thinking about possible answers to your questions.

Text Page 4: *Do You Like to Ski?*

FOCUS

> Review of:
> - *Don't and doesn't*
> - *Like to*
> - Agent nouns
> - Negative forms of the verb *to be*

GETTING READY

1. Review short answers with *don't* and *doesn't*.

   a. Have students look at the left-hand box at the top of the page as you ask questions about people in the class, using each pronoun and the simple present tense. Have students respond with negative short answers. For example:

Teacher	Student
Do you speak (German)?	No, I don't.
Do you and (Mary) wear glasses?	No, we don't.
Do I live in (Tokyo)?	No, you don't.
Do (Bill) and (Bob) drive too fast?	No, they don't.
Does (Barbara) study in (London)?	No, she doesn't.
Does (Tom) like to cook?	No, he doesn't.

   b. Call on students to make up other questions such as those above; have other students answer.

2. Review short answers with the verb *to be*.

   a. Have students look at the right-hand box at the top of the page.* Ask questions about people in the class, using each pronoun and the verb *to be*. Have students answer with negative short answers. For example:

Teacher	Student
Are you married?	No, I'm not.
Are you and (Carol) sisters?	No, we aren't.
Am I a student?	No, you aren't.
Are (Bill) and (Bob) teachers?	No, they aren't.
Is (Ted) a truck driver?	No, he isn't.
Is (Betty) a doctor?	No, she isn't.

   b. Call on students to make up other questions such as those above; have other students answer.

INTRODUCING THE MODEL

1. Have students look at the model illustration.
2. Set the scene: "Two people are riding on a ski lift. They just met each other."

---

*The following negative forms are presented:

he isn't	we aren't
she isn't	you aren't
it isn't	they aren't

Equally correct alternatives are:

he's not	we're not
she's not	you're not
it's not	they're not

3. Present the model.

4. Full-Class Choral Repetition.

5. Ask students if they have any questions; check understanding of vocabulary.

6. Group Choral Repetition.

7. Choral Conversation.

8. Call on one or two pairs of students to present the dialog.

   (For additional practice, do Choral Conversation in small groups or by rows.)

SIDE BY SIDE EXERCISES

Examples

> 1. A. Does Jim like to dance?
>   B. No, he doesn't. He isn't a very good dancer.
>
> 2. A. Does Rita like to sing?
>   B. No, she doesn't. She isn't a very good singer.
>
> 3. A. Do Mr. and Mrs. Brown like to skate?
>   B. No, they don't. They aren't very good skaters.

1. **Exercise 1:** Call on two students to present the dialog. Then do Choral Repetition and Choral Conversation Practice.

2. **Exercise 2:** Same as above.

3. **Exercises 3–9:**

> **New vocabulary:** 3. *skater* 4. *typist* 6. *swimmer* 8. *athlete* 9. *cook* (n)

Either Full-Class Practice or Pair Practice.

WORKBOOK

Pages 6–7 (Exercises E, F)

EXPANSION ACTIVITIES

1. Is That True?

a. Write statements such as those below on word cards.

1. Mary dances beautifully.
2. Bob doesn't play tennis very well.
3. Shirley and her sister type very quickly.
4. You're a very good student.
5. You play sports very well.
6. Rita doesn't sing very well.
7. Mr. Brown skates very badly.
8. I sing beautifully.
9. You and your friends ski very well.
10. Helen Smith teaches very well.
11. You compose beautiful music.
12. Judy writes great books.
13. Michael cooks very well.

b. Put this conversational model on the board:

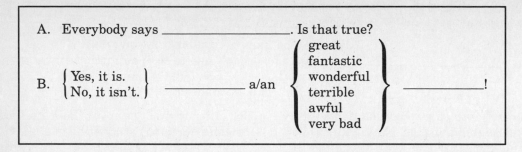

A. Everybody says _____. Is that true?

B. { Yes, it is. } _____ a/an { great fantastic wonderful terrible awful very bad } _____!
   { No, it isn't. }

c. Give the cards to pairs of students. Have students create conversations, using the model on the board, and then present them to the class. Students may choose to agree or disagree with the first speaker. For example:

   A. Everybody says Mary dances beautifully. Is that true?
   B. Yes, it is. She's a wonderful dancer!
      or
      No, it isn't. She's an awful dancer!

2. *Review Professions*

a. Write on the board:

He's/She's a/an _____.
They're _____s.

b. Have students listen as you read the job descriptions of the people below. After each description, have students tell the profession, using the sentence models on the board. Have students answer chorally and individually.

1. Robert plays the violin in concerts. (violinist)
2. Mr. Barnaby drives trucks between New York and Miami. (truck driver)
3. Larry plays tennis all over the world. (tennis player)
4. Judy and Bill Jones cook in a very good restaurant. (cooks/chefs)
5. Mr. Schultz repairs televisions. (TV repairman)
6. Natasha helps the doctors take care of people in the hospital. (nurse)
7. Walter Miller acts in plays and movies. (actor)
8. Maria Miller, Walter's wife, acts in plays and movies, too. (actress)
9. Toshi bakes bread, cakes, and special desserts. (baker)
10. Nancy translates Russian. (translator)
11. Mr. Harris teaches in a school. (teacher)
12. Patty Brown drives a bus in Chicago. (bus driver)
13 Michael and his brother Carl fix broken sinks. (plumbers)
14. Mr. Smith and his son Peter fix cars. (mechanics)
15. Barbara paints houses for a living. (painter)
16. Boris plays chess in countries all over the world. (chess player)
17. Carol types for a company downtown. (typist)
18. Dr. Sherman takes care of sick dogs and cats. (veterinarian)

c. Find out what other professions your students are interested in. Have students use their dictionaries to find out the names of these occupations and tell what the people do.

3. Students Tell about Themselves

a. Set the scene by telling about yourself or about a person on the board. For example:

"This is Mary. Mary likes to swim, and she's a good swimmer. She likes to type, but she isn't a very good typist. She doesn't like to cook because she isn't a very good cook. She likes to play the piano, and she plays whenever she can."

b. Divide students into pairs. Have students interview each other to find out about their likes and dislikes and related abilities. Have each student tell the class about the student he or she interviewed.

Variation:

You can do this as a writing activity. For homework, have students write about themselves: their likes, dislikes, and related abilities.

4. Vocabulary Review: Finish the Sentence

a. Write the following words on the board:

athletic	lazy	ocean	racket	typist
fall	music	paper	recipe	words

b. Say the sentences below. Have students use the appropriate word on the board to complete each sentence.

1. I can't play tennis because I don't have a _____.
2. Peter can't type because he doesn't have any _____.
3. We can't sing that song because we don't know the _____.
4. We can't dance because there isn't any _____.
5. I don't like to skate because I always _____.
6. My daughter doesn't like to swim in the _____.
7. I'm sorry. I can't make that cake for dessert because I don't have the _____.
8. I don't like to play sports because I'm not _____.
9. Beverly doesn't like to study because she's _____.
10. Alan's boss fired him because he's a terrible _____.

5. Classroom Interviews

a. On an index card, have each student write three things that he or she likes to do. For example:

> I like to swim.
> I like to watch TV.
> I like to play tennis.

b. Collect the cards and distribute them randomly to all the students in the class.

c. Have students interview others in the class to match the correct person with each card, that is, to find out which student likes to do the three activities written on each card.

d. When the interviews are completed, call on students to tell about the others in the class, based on their interviews. For example:

> Bob likes to swim.
> He likes to watch TV.
> And he likes to play tennis.

Text Pages 5–6

READING: *Practicing*

FOCUS

Review:
- Simple present tense
- Present continuous tense
- Subject pronouns
- Object pronouns
- Possessive adjectives

NEW VOCABULARY

ballet dancer
coach (n)
dance ballet
dance teacher
football coach
music teacher
professional
stay after
tennis coach

PREVIEWING THE STORY (optional)

Have students talk about the story title and/or illustrations. Introduce new vocabulary.

READING THE STORY

1. Have students read silently, or follow along silently as the story is read aloud by you, by one or more students, or on the tape.
2. Ask students if they have any questions; check understanding of vocabulary.
3. Check students' comprehension, using some or all of the following questions:

   a. What am I doing?
   b. How often do I practice?
   c. What does my tennis coach tell me?
   d. What do my friends tell me?
   e. What do I want to be when I grow up?

   f. What's Jimmy doing?
   g. How often does he practice?
   h. What does his football coach tell him?
   i. What do his friends tell him?
   j. What does he want to be when he grows up?

   k. What's Susan doing?
   l. How often does she practice?
   m. What does her music teacher tell her?
   n. What do her friends tell her?
   o. What does she want to be when she grows up?

   p. What are Patty and Melissa doing?
   q. How often do they practice?
   r. What does their dance teacher tell them?
   s. What do their friends tell them?
   t. What do they want to be when they grow up?

CHECK-UP

Q & A

1. Call on a pair of students to present the model.
2. Have students work in pairs to create new dialogs.
3. Call on pairs to present their new dialogs to the class.

Listening

Have students complete the exercises as you play the tape or read the following:

Listen and choose the best answer.

1. What are you doing? (b)
2. Do you swim very often? (b)
3. Are you a good cook? (a)
4. What's Tom cooking? (b)
5. Who cooks in your family? (a)
6. Do they like to study? (b)
7. Does he want to be a violinist? (a)
8. Are you and your brother busy this afternoon? (b)
9. Does Mrs. King like to swim? (b)
10. What's Peter reading? (a)

IN YOUR OWN WORDS

1. Make sure students understand the instructions.
2. Have students do the activity as written homework, using a dictionary for any new words they wish to use.
3. Have students present and discuss what they have written, in pairs or as a class.

Text Pages 7–8: *How Often?*

FOCUS

- Review of pronouns
- Contrast of the simple present and present continuous tenses

GETTING READY

1. Review pronouns.

   a. Write on the board:

   > My $\left\{ \begin{array}{l} \text{friend} \\ \text{friends} \end{array} \right\}$ —————— $\left\{ \begin{array}{l} \text{likes} \\ \text{like} \end{array} \right\}$ to visit me here in ——————.
   >
   > When —————— $\left\{ \begin{array}{l} \text{comes} \\ \text{come} \end{array} \right\}$ to visit, I always take ———— to ———— favorite $\left\{ \begin{array}{l} \text{museum.} \\ \text{restaurant.} \\ \text{theater.} \end{array} \right\}$

   b. Set the scene: "My friend Tom likes to visit me here in (name of your city). When he comes to visit, I always take him to his favorite restaurant."

   c. Have students use this model to review other pronouns. Ask students, "What about your friend(s) ——————?" Students can refer to the box at the top of text page 7 for the pronoun. For example:

      A. What about your friend Sally?
      B. My friend Sally likes to visit me here in ——————.
         When she comes to visit, I always take her to her favorite museum.

      A. What about your friends Joe and Judy?
      B. My friends Joe and Judy like to visit me here in ——————.
         When they come to visit, I always take them to their favorite theater.

   d. Change *my* to *our* in the model on the board. Have students make all the necessary changes as they tell about *our friend(s)* —————— *and* ——————.

INTRODUCING THE MODEL

There are two model conversations. Introduce and practice each separately. For each model:

1. Have students look at the model illustration.
2. Set the scene:

   1st model: "Two friends are talking. One of them is making a phone call."
   2nd model: "Two men are sitting in the park and talking."
3. Present the model.
4. Full-Class Choral Repetition.
5. Ask students if they have any questions; check understanding of new vocabulary: *how often, all the time.*

   #### Language Note

   Who are you calling? The pronoun *who* rather than *whom* is widely used in informal conversation. The pronoun *whom* is used in more formal speech.

6. Group Choral Repetition.

7. Choral Conversation.

8. Call on one or two pairs of students to present the dialog.

9. After the 1st model,

    a. Go over the alternative vocabulary at the bottom of the page. Review the days of the week and months of the year.

    b. Introduce the new expressions:

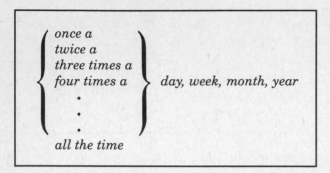

    c. Have several pairs of students present the dialog again, using alternative vocabulary in place of *every Sunday evening.*

10. After the 2nd model, have several pairs of students present the dialog again, using alternative vocabulary in place of *all the time.*

SIDE BY SIDE EXERCISES

Students can use any time expression they wish to complete these dialogs.

Examples

1. A. Who is Mrs. Lopez calling?
   B. She's calling her daughter in San Francisco.
   A. How often does she call her?
   B. She calls her (every week).

2. A. Who are you writing to?
   B. I'm writing to my uncle.
   A. How often do you write to him?
   B. I write to him (once a month).

1. **Exercise 1:** Call on two students to present the dialog. Then do Choral Repetition and Choral Conversation Practice.

2. **Exercise 2:** Same as above.

3. **Exercises 3–9:**

New vocabulary:	4. *army*	7. *electric bill*

Language Note

    Who is Mr. Davis arguing with? (Exercise 5): The use of a preposition at the end of a sentence is also common in informal speech. A formal version of this question would be *With whom is Mr. Davis arguing?*

Culture Note

Exercise 9:   Little Red Riding Hood is the name of a well-known English folk tale about a little girl who wears a red hood when she goes to visit her grandmother in her house in the woods. In the story, a clever wolf pretends to be the grandmother and nearly succeeds in eating Little Red Riding Hood.

Either Full-Class Practice or Pair Practice.

Whenever possible, after each exercise ask students to compare their own experience with that of the people in the exercise. For example, after Exercise 3 ask "How about you? Do you visit your neighbors?" After Exercise 4 ask "How often do you write letters?" After Exercise 5 ask "Do you argue with your landlord?"

4. **Exercise 10:**   Have students use the model as a guide to create their own conversations, using vocabulary of their choice. Encourage students to use dictionaries to find new words they want to use. This exercise can be done orally in class or for written homework. If you assign it for homework, you should do one example in class to make sure students understand what's expected. Have students present their conversations in class the next day.

WORKBOOK

Pages 7–9 (Exercises G, H, I)

EXPANSION ACTIVITIES

1. *Review Pronouns: A Story about Peggy and John*

    a. Put the following on the board:

    b. Set the scene: "I want to tell you about my friends Peggy and John."

    c. Read each sentence below while pointing to the faces on the board. Have students listen and repeat each sentence, changing all the nouns to pronouns.

    Ex.   Peggy and John are married.
    (They're married.)

    1. Peggy likes John.
        (She likes him.)
    2. John likes Peggy.
        (He likes her.)
    3. Peggy and John live in Canada.
        (They live in Canada.)
    4. Peggy and John's last name is Jones.
        (Their last name is Jones.)
    5. Peggy met John at a party.
        (She met him at a party.)

    6. John liked Peggy right away.
        (He liked her right away.)
    7. John and Peggy got married at Peggy's parents' house.
        (They got married at her parents' house.)
    8. On Peggy's last birthday, John gave Peggy a watch.
        (On her last birthday, he gave her a watch.)
    9. On John's last birthday, Peggy gave John a new coat.
        (On his last birthday, she gave him a new coat.)

2. Role Play: At the Doctor's Office

a. Put this conversational model and the word cues below on the board:

> A. How often do you _____?
>
> B. I _____ { all the time / every _____ / once a _____ / twice a _____ / _____ times a _____ } .
>
> A. I see. And how often do you _____?
> B. I _____.
> A. Well, you don't seem to have any serious medical problems.
>   I'll see you next year.

Cues:

exercise	go to bed late
take vitamins	listen to loud music
drink _____	go to the dentist
eat rich desserts	

b. Set the scene: "You're at the doctor's office for your annual physical examination."

c. Call on pairs of students to role play the conversation. Speaker A is the *doctor*. Speaker B is the *patient*. For example:

> A. How often do you exercise?
> B. I exercise once a week.
> A. I see. And how often do you take vitamins?
> B. I take vitamins every morning.
> A. Well, you don't seem to have any serious medical problems.
>   I'll see you next year.

Encourage students to expand the dialog in any way they wish.

3. Vocabulary Review: Mystery Word

a. Divide the class into pairs.

b. Give each pair a card with a *mystery word* on it. Possibilities include:

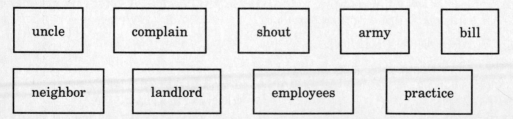

uncle	complain	shout	army	bill

neighbor	landlord	employees	practice

c. Have each pair create a sentence in which that word is in final position. For example:

My aunt's husband is my _____ . (uncle)
Before you leave the hotel, don't forget to pay the _____ . (bill)

d. One student from the pair then reads aloud the sentence with the final word missing. The other pairs of students try to guess the missing word.

This can be done as a game, where each pair scores a point for identifying the correct *mystery word*. The pair with the most points wins the game.

4. *Little Red Riding Hood*

Little Red Riding Hood appears in Exercise 9 in the student text. If you think your students would be interested, go to the library, find the story of Little Red Riding Hood, and read it to the class. Possible follow-up activities:

a. Call on students to retell the story.

b. Read the story and have students write it as best they can remember it.

c. Have students tell the class famous folk tales from their countries.

Text Page 9

ON YOUR OWN: *Getting to Know Each Other*

FOCUS

> Present tense review: Students talk about themselves

ON YOUR OWN ACTIVITY

There are four topics of conversation, with suggested questions under each. For each topic:

1. Go over the question and introduce new vocabulary.

> **New vocabulary:**   1. *What do you do?*   4. *interests, free time*

Culture Note

> *What do you do?* This question is commonly used to find out what someone's profession is. The importance of this question in U.S. culture reflects the value of work as a means of establishing one's identity in a group.

Have students repeat each question chorally.

2. Tell about yourself; then ask one or two students. For example:

   "I'm from Tokyo, but now I live in Paris."
   "Where are you from?"
   "Where do you live now?"

3. Divide the class into pairs. Have students interview each other, using the questions in the book. Have each student take notes to help remember the other's answers.

4. Call on several students to report back to the class about the people they interviewed.

5. For homework, have students write 10–15 sentences about themselves and 10–15 sentences about the person they interviewed.

EXPANSION ACTIVITIES

1. Silent Letters

Write some or all of the words below on the board. Have students try to find the silent letter or letters in each word:

> knit (*k*nit)   neighbor (nei*gh*bor)
> plumber (plum*b*er)   ballet (balle*t*)
> daughter (dau*gh*ter)   right (ri*gh*t)
> knife (*k*nife)   wrong (*w*rong)

2. *Who Is Your Favorite?*

Have students talk about their favorite writers, singers, painters, actors, actresses, and composers.

a. Put on the board:

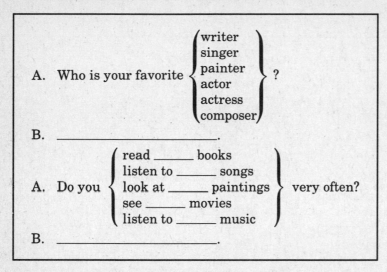

b. Have pairs of students create conversations based on the model. This can be Full-Class Practice or Pair Practice. Examples:

A. Who is your favorite singer?
B. Tom Jones.
A. Do you listen to his songs very often?
B. Yes, I do. I listen to them every day.

A. Who is your favorite actress?
B. Sophia Loren.
A. Do you see her movies very often?
B. Yes. I see them whenever I can.

WORKBOOK ANSWER KEY AND LISTENING SCRIPTS

Page 1 A. WHAT'S HAPPENING?

1. What's, drinking
   She's drinking
2. Where's, going
   She's going
3. What's, planting
   He's planting
4. What are
   eating
   We're eating
5. Where are, moving
   They're moving
6. What are, baking
   I'm baking
7. What are, buying
   They're buying
8. Where's, swimming
   He's swimming

Page 2 B. ON THE PHONE

1. are
   I'm cooking
   Is
   he is, He's taking
2. What are
   we're
3. Are
   They're
   are
   is studying
   are watching
4. Is
   He's working
   She's
   What's she
   She's fixing

Page 4 C. YOU DECIDE: *Why Is Today Different?*

1. clean, I'm cleaning
   . . . .
2. wears, he's wearing
   . . . .
3. work, we're working
   . . . .
4. argues, he's arguing
   . . . .
5. sends, he's sending
   . . . .
6. studies, she's studying
   . . . .

7. take, they're taking
   . . . .
8. watches, he's/she's watching
   . . . .
9. writes, he's writing
   . . . .
10. gets up, she's getting up
    . . . .
11. drink, they're drinking
    . . . .
12. goes, she's going
    . . . .
13. smiles, he's smiling
    . . . .

Page 5 D. WHAT ARE THEY SAYING?

1. Does, play
2. Does, live
3. Do, get up
4. Do, go
5. Does, like
6. Do, watch
7. Does she bake
8. Do you walk
9. Does he speak
10. Do they work
11. Does he have
12. Do they complain
13. Do you drink
14. Does she worry

Page 6 E. WHAT'S THE WORD?

1. don't, isn't
   he's
2. isn't
   sings
   She's
3. doesn't
   I'm, drive
4. isn't, doesn't
   swimmer

NEW VOCABULARY

a lot
audience
behind
best friend
bet (v)
black eye
boat
clothing
Colosseum
come home
cover (v)
daily
daily exercises
demonstrator
exam
excited (adj)
experience
find out
flight
interview (n)
interviewer
job interview
lecture (n)
lines
magic trick
magician

Mediterranean
monument
mountain
one day
pool
postcard
prepare
prepared (adj)
realize
rip (v)
run away
scared (adj)
sleep well
souvenir
take pictures
tourist
travel around
Vatican
wave (v)
work hard
wreck (v)
yet

I bet
look over *his* shoulder

Past Tense Verb Forms

Irregular		Regular	
break	– broke	burn	– burned
buy	– bought	clean	– cleaned
come	– came	cover	– covered
cut	– cut	cry	– cried
do	– did	dance	– danced
eat	– ate	finish	– finished
fall	– fell	look	– looked
forget	– forgot	practice	– practiced
get	– got	prepare	– prepared
go	– went	rip	– ripped
have	– had	shave	– shaved
hurt	– hurt	shout	– shout
leave	– left	stay	– stayed
lose	– lost	study	– studied
meet	– met		
read	– read		
ride	– rode	***-ing* Forms**	
run	– ran	arguing	
see	– saw	baking	
send	– sent	dancing	
sleep	– slept	playing	
swim	– swam	practicing	
take	– took	preparing	
teach	– taught	reading	
write	– wrote	shaving	
		skiing	
am, is, are – was, were		waiting	

LANGUAGE NOTES

1. **Use of the Simple Past Tense**

   The simple past tense is used to describe completed events that occurred in the past, such as:

   a. Events that occurred at a particular point in time. For example:

   > *I got up at 7 o'clock this morning.*
   > *Sally broke her leg.*

   b. Events that took place over a period of time. For example:

   > *Henry cleaned his apartment all day.*

   The simple past tense can also be used with appropriate time expressions to describe past habitual activity. For example:

   > *She always drove too fast.*
   > *They went to the beach every summer.*

2. **Use of the Past Continuous Tense**

   The past continuous tense is commonly used to show the duration of a past activity in contrast with a particular point in time. For example:

   > *John broke his arm while he was playing tennis.*
   > *I was cooking dinner when Bob came home.*

3. **Pronunciation of Past Tense Verbs Ending in *-ted* and *-ded***

   When a verb ending in *t* or *d* takes the regular past tense *-ed* ending, an additional syllable is formed at the end of the word. For example:

   > *shout –shouted*
   > *paint –painted*

Text Page 12: *Did They Sleep Well Last Night?*

FOCUS

> Review of the past tense:
> - Regular and irregular verbs
> - The verb *to be: was/were*
> - Questions with *did*
> - Affirmative short answers

GETTING READY

Review the past tense.

1. Practice listening for the *-ed* ending.

   a. Write on the board:

      > every day   yesterday

   b. Read the statements below one or more times and have students respond by saying "every day" when they hear a verb in the present tense and "yesterday" when they hear a verb in the past tense. For example:

"I work."	"every day"
"I worked."	"yesterday"

1. She works.	7. He studied.
2. He worked.	8. She plays the piano.
3. They worked.	9. We played baseball.
4. They work.	10. They need some books.
5. We study.	11. I study.
6. I bake a cake.	12. She needed a loaf of bread.

2. Practice forming sentences which contrast verb endings in the simple present and simple past tenses.

   a. Write on the board:

I He She We You They	work study clean – apartment	yesterday. every day.

   b. Call on students to form sentences with these words. For each student, point to one word in each column; the student then makes a sentence using these words. For example:

1. (She) (study) (every day)	→	"She studies every day."
2. (He) (study) (yesterday)	→	"He studied yesterday."
3. (They) (work) (yesterday)	→	"They worked yesterday."

3. Review a few irregular verbs in the past tense.

  a. Using the same columns on the board from 2 above, change the verbs to *teach* and *write*.

  b. Review the past tense forms *taught* and *wrote*.

  c. Again, have students form sentences, using one word from each column.

4. Review the past tense of the verb *to be*.

  a. Write on the board:

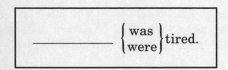

  b. Say each pronoun and have students form sentences using the correct verb. Have students respond chorally and individually. For example:

> (He): "He was tired."
> (They): "They were tired."

INTRODUCING THE MODEL

1. Have students look at the model illustration.
2. Set the scene: "Two people are talking about Henry."
3. Present the model.
4. Full-Class Choral Repetition.
5. Ask students if they have any questions; check understanding of new vocabulary: *sleep well.*
6. Group Choral Repetition.
7. Choral Conversation.
8. Call on one or two pairs of students to present the dialog.

  (For additional practice, do Choral Conversation in small groups or by rows.)

SIDE BY SIDE EXERCISES

Examples

> 1. A. Did you sleep well last night?
>   B. Yes, I did. I was VERY tired.
>   A. Why? What did you do yesterday?
>   B. I studied English all day.
>
> 2. A. Did Gloria sleep well last night?
>   B. Yes, she did. She was VERY tired.
>   A. Why? What did she do yesterday?
>   B. She worked hard all day.

1. **Exercise 1:** Review the verb *study–studied*. Call on two students to present the dialog. Then do Choral Repetition and Choral Conversation Practice.

2. **Exercise 2:** Review the verb *work–worked*. Introduce the expression *work hard*. Same as above.

3. **Exercises 3–8:**

> **Verb review:** 3. *wash–washed*   4. *teach–taught*   5. *look–looked*
> 6. *ride–rode*   7. *write–wrote*   8. *meet–met*

Either Full-Class Practice or Pair Practice.

4. **Exercise 9:** Have students use the model as a guide to create their own conversations, using vocabulary of their choice. (They can use any names and activities they wish.) Encourage students to use dictionaries to find new words they want to use. This exercise can be done orally in class or for written homework. If you assign it for homework, you should do one example in class to make sure students understand what's expected. Have students present their conversations in class the next day.

WORKBOOK

Pages 10–12 (Exercises A, B, C)

Exercise Note

Workbook p. 10: Students complete the story with any vocabulary they wish. Have students compare their endings to *the nightmare*.

EXPANSION ACTIVITIES

1. **Role Play:** *Talking about Dreams*

   a. Write on the board:

   > A. I had an incredible dream last night.
   > B. Oh, really? What did you dream?
   > A. I dreamed that _____.
   > B. What a dream!
   > A. How about you? What did YOU dream last night?
   > B. I dreamed that _____.

   b. Give each student a word card with one of the verbs below on it. (More than one student can have the same verb.)

   > | | | | | | |
   > |---|---|---|---|---|---|
   > | wash | study | look | write | clean | see |
   > | work | teach | ride | meet | was/were | |

   c. Call on pairs of students to create conversations based on the model on the board. Students must use the verbs on their cards to describe their dreams. Encourage students to be lively and imaginative. For example:

   > Student A (wash)
   > Student B (meet)

   > A. I had an incredible dream last night.
   > B. Oh, really? What did you dream?
   > A. I dreamed that I washed a hundred shirts and I was so tired that I slept for two days.
   > B. What a dream!
   > A. How about you? What did YOU dream last night?
   > B. I dreamed that I met the President and he asked my opinion about world problems.

2. **Tell More about Situation 8**

Have students look at the illustration for Exercise 8. Ask students the questions below. These questions allow students to use their imaginations to *tell you more* about the people in the situation.

> Did the President sleep well last night?
> What did he do yesterday?
> Who did the President meet?
> What did they talk about?

3. **Discussion: Hard Work**

Many of the situations on text page 12 deal with hard work. Have students talk about hard work they or others have done. Possible questions are:

> Did you work hard (yesterday/last night/over the weekend)?
> What did you do?
> Do you think that's hard work? Why?
> How did you feel afterward?
> Did (your friends/your roommate/your brother) work hard, too?
> What did (he/she/they) do?

Text Page 13: *Did Mrs. Clark Shout at Her Son?*

FOCUS

> Review of the past tense:
> * More regular and irregular verbs
> * *Yes/no* questions and short answers with *did*
> * Review of negative statements with the verb *to be*

GETTING READY

Contrast *did* and *was/were*.

1. Write on the board:

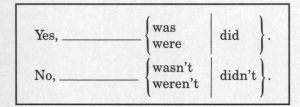

2. Make up questions, such as those below, that will pertain to your students' experience. Pick questions that will allow students to practice all the forms on the board. Read each question and have students respond chorally and/or individually.

   a. Was it (sunny) yesterday?
   b. Did it (rain) yesterday?
   c. Were (Bob) and (Jane) late for class today?
   d. Did (Mary) miss class last week?
   e. Were (you) on time this morning?
   f. Did (Alice) and (George) ride their bicycles to class today?
   g. Were we at school last (Wednesday)?
   h. Was (Gloria) at the beach yesterday?
   i. Did you sleep for (15) hours last night?
   j. Was (John) tired this morning?
   k. Did (Katherine) look for a new apartment last weekend?
   l. Did we study (French) in class last week?

INTRODUCING THE MODEL

There are two model conversations. Introduce and practice each separately. For each model:

1. Have students look at the model illustration in the book.
2. Set the scene:

1st model:	"Two people are talking about Mrs. Clark."
2nd model:	"Two people are talking about Sam's exam."

3. Present the model.
4. Full-Class Choral Repetition.
5. Ask students if they have any questions; check understanding of new vocabulary:

   2nd model: *do well on his English exam, prepared*

6. Group Choral Repetition.

7. Choral Conversation.

8. Call on one or two pairs of students to present the dialog.

   (For additional practice, do Choral Conversation in small groups or by rows.)

SIDE BY SIDE EXERCISES

Examples

> 1. A. Did Marylou cry a lot when her dog ran away?
>   B. Yes, she did. She was upset.
>
> 2. A. Did Katherine sleep well last night?
>   B. No, she didn't. She wasn't tired.

1. **Exercise 1:** Introduce the new expressions *a lot, run away.* Call on two students to present the dialog. Then do Choral Repetition and Choral Conversation Practice.

2. **Exercise 2:** Same as above.

3. **Exercises 3–8:**

> **New vocabulary:**   3. *lecture*   5. *lines*   7. *cover* (v), *scared*

Either Full-Class Practice or Pair Practice.

WORKBOOK

Pages 12–15 (Exercises D, E, F)

> *Exercise Note*
>
> Workbook p. 14: For additional oral practice with Exercise F, have students act out the conversations.

EXPANSION ACTIVITIES

1. *Role Play: Model Conversations and Situations 1, 2, 3, 5, 7*

   a. Review these verb forms from text page 13.

> **Model conversations**
> | | |
> |---|---|
> | *shout – shouted* | *do well – did well* |
>
> **Exercises**
> | | |
> |---|---|
> | 1. *cry – cried* | 2. *sleep – slept* |
> | *run – ran* | |
> | 3. *fall asleep – fell asleep* | 4. *finish – finished* |
> | 5. *forget – forgot* | 6. *have – had* |
> | 7. *cover – covered* | 8. *leave – left* |

b. Divide the class into pairs and have each pair prepare a short role play to present to the class. Use both model conversations and Exercises 1, 2, 3, 5, 7. Have students pretend to be the people in the situations and create a possible 4–6 line dialog based on the situation. Encourage students to use their imaginations to embellish the dialogs. Suggest that students begin their dialogs like this: "Hi, _____. What's new?" For example:

(Situation 3)

A. Hi, (Mary). What's new?
B. Well, I went to a lecture yesterday.
A. That's nice. How was it?
B. It was very boring. In fact, it was so boring that I fell asleep.
A. Really?
B. Yes. The chairs were very comfortable, and the speaker was terrible!

2. **Review Verbs with Visuals**

Use your own visuals or *Side by Side* Picture Cards 18–41, 124–139, and 164–171 to review verbs in the past tense.

a. Hold up a visual and ask a student:

"What did _____ do (yesterday/last night . . .)?"

For additional practice, you can do Choral Repetition.

You can use any appropriate time expression or name in your questions. For example:

"What did (Bill) do last weekend?"
"What did (your friends) do yesterday?"
"What did (Sally) do this morning?"
"What did (you) do today?"
"What did (we) do last week?"

b. Give the visuals to students and have them ask and answer questions in the past tense.

3. **Pronunciation Exercise: The Boys at Dover Academy**

Use the story below to have students practice past tense verbs in -*ted* and -*ded*.

a. Put on the board:

Peter	Richard	Sam	Nelson
painted	didn't feel well	started	went
	rested		needed

Pat	Walter	Frank
planted	went	went
	wanted	fainted

b. Set the scene: "The boys at Dover Academy are always very busy."
c. Point to the appropriate cue as you tell each part of the story below.

"Last Saturday afternoon . . .
   Peter painted his room.
   Richard didn't feel very well, so he rested in bed.
   Sam started to study for a history exam.
   Nelson went to the store because he needed a new notebook.
   Pat planted flowers in front of the school.
   Walter went to the library because he wanted to be by himself.
   Frank went jogging in the hot sun and fainted."

d. Ask questions about the story. You can pause as you tell it and ask questions, or you can wait until the end. Then call on one or two students to retell the whole story.

e. As an optional writing assignment, have students write the story, using only the cues on the board.

4. *Vocabulary Review: Finish the Sentence*

a. Write the following words on the board:

angry	hungry	on time	scared	tired
bored	nervous	prepared	thirsty	upset

b. Say the sentences below. Have students complete each sentence with the appropriate word on the board.

1. He drank two bottles of soda because he was very . . .
2. I didn't know the answers on the test because I wasn't . . .
3. Kathy didn't want to go into that dark room herself because she was . . .
4. Bob fell asleep in class because he was . . .
5. I didn't have any lunch today, and now I'm . . .
6. Class began at nine. I arrived at nine thirty. I wasn't . . .
7. My little brother cried because he was . . .
8. It rained all day yesterday. I stayed home and didn't do anything. I was . . .
9. Your big exam is tomorrow. Are you feeling . . .?
10. Paul had an accident with his father's car. His father was very . . .

5. *Role Play: Guess How They're Feeling*

a. Write the following words on the board:

angry	bored	hungry	nervous	scared	thirsty	tired

b. Divide the class into pairs.

c. Give each pair a situation card. Possibilities include:

> You're at the movies, and you're talking about the movie you're watching.

> You and a friend are at a restaurant, and the service is very slow tonight.

> You and a friend are at a lecture.

> You and a friend are sitting in the waiting room at the doctor's office.

> You and a friend are talking before English class.

d. Give each pair a card with one of the *feeling* words from the board written on it.

e. Have each pair prepare a short role play based on their situation and then act it out for the class, according to the *feeling* on their card.

f. The rest of the class has to guess what was on the card:

"They're angry."
"They're nervous."
　etc.

Text Pages 14–15: *How Did John Break His Arm?*

FOCUS

> Review of the past continuous tense

GETTING READY

Use your own visuals or *Side by Side* Picture Cards for verbs to review the past continuous tense.

1. Hold up visuals and ask students questions in the past continuous tense. For example:

   (Side by Side Picture Card 25)   A. What were they doing last night?
                                                   B. They were playing cards.

   (Side by Side Picture Card 18)   A. What was he doing last night?
                                                   B. He was reading.

2. Hold up visuals and have pairs of students ask and answer, using the past continuous tense.

INTRODUCING THE MODEL

1. Have students look at the model illustration.
2. Set the scene: "Two people are talking about John's accident."
3. Present the model.
4. Full-Class Choral Repetition.
5. Ask students if they have any questions; check understanding of new vocabulary: *break–broke*.
6. Group Choral Repetition.
7. Choral Conversation.
8. Call on one or two pairs of students to present the dialog.

   (For additional practice, do Choral Conversation in small groups or by rows.)

SIDE BY SIDE EXERCISES

Examples

> 1. A. How did Sally break her leg?
>   B. She broke it while she was skiing down a mountain.
>
> 2. A. How did Martin lose his wallet?
>   B. He lost it while he was playing baseball with his son.

1. **Exercise 1:** Introduce the new expression *down a mountain*. Call on two students to present the dialog. Then do Choral Repetition and Choral Conversation Practice.

2. **Exercise 2:** Review the irregular verb *lose–lost*. Same as above.

3. **Exercises 3–10:**

Language Notes

Exercise 3:   The verb *meet* has many meanings. The three meanings described below are sometimes confused by students.

     a.   To become acquainted with for the first time. For example: *Peggy met her husband while she was reading in the library one day.*

     b.   To come upon, or encounter. For example: *I met an old friend on the bus recently.*

     c.   To get together at an appointed time or place. For example: *I'll meet you at 10 o'clock in front of the library.*

Exercise 6:   A black eye is a bruised eye that can result from a blow to the eye.

Either Full-class Practice or Pair Practice.

WORKBOOK

Page 16

HOW ABOUT YOU?

1. Divide the class into pairs. Have students tell each other how they met special people in their lives.
2. Have students report back to the class about the person they talked with. For example:

> "Jane met her friend Susan while she was on vacation at the beach. Susan was staying in the house next to Jane."

> "Bill met his wife at a party. Everybody was dancing, and Bill asked her to dance."

EXPANSION ACTIVITIES

1. Role Play: I Saw You

Have pairs of students role play the conversation below. Use your own visuals or *Side by Side* Picture Cards as cues for community locations. Students can use any vocabulary they wish to finish the dialog as long as the verb is in the past continuous tense.

     a.   Briefly review some or all of the locations in the community below, using visuals if possible. Say each word and then have students tell what people usually do in that location. For example:

> "library": read/study/borrow books

airport	clinic	hospital	playground
bakery	concert hall	laundromat	police station
bank	courthouse	library	post office
bus station	department store	movie theater	school
butcher shop	doctor's office	museum	shopping mall
cafeteria	drug store	park	supermarket
candy store	gas station	pet shop	train station
	hardware store		zoo

b. Write on the board:

> A. Weren't you at the _____ yesterday?
> B. Yes, I was. How did you know?
> A. I was there, too. I was _____. I saw you, but I guess you didn't see me.
> B. I'm sorry I didn't see you. I was _____, and I was in a hurry.

c. Call on pairs of students to role play the dialog. For each pair, signal a location in the community with a visual or word card. For example:

Cue: *department store*

> A. Weren't you at the department store yesterday?
> B. Yes, I was. How did you know?
> A. I was there, too. I was (looking for a new coat). I saw you, but I guess you didn't see me.
> B. I'm sorry I didn't see you. I was (buying a birthday present for my girlfriend), and I was in a hurry.

2. A Bad Day

a. Write the following conversational model on the board:

> A. I had a bad day today.
> B. Why? What happened?
> A. _____ while _____.
> B. That's a shame!

b. Write the following cues on the board or on word cards:

> cut myself   forget _____
> lose my _____   fall asleep
> rip my _____   fall down
> spill _____   burn _____

c. Have pairs of students create conversations based on the word cues and the model on the board. For example:

> A. I had a bad day today.
> B. Why? What happened?
> A. I cut myself while I was cooking dinner.
> B. That's a shame!

> A. I had a bad day today.
> B. Why? What happened?
> A. I lost my homework while I was walking to school.
> B. That's a shame!

Text Pages 16–18

READING: *Difficult Experiences*

FOCUS

Review:
* Simple past tense (regular and irregular verbs)
* Past continuous tense

NEW VOCABULARY

at the back of	experience
audience	look over *his* shoulder
behind	realize
demonstrator	wave

PREVIEWING THE STORY (optional)

Have students talk about the story title and/or illustrations. Introduce new vocabulary.

READING THE STORY

1. Have students read silently, or follow along silently as the story is read aloud by you, by one or more students, or on the tape.
2. Ask students if they have any questions; check understanding of vocabulary.

   Culture Note

   Demonstrators often go to listen to a politician's speech. During the speech, they shout and disrupt the politician because they disagree and are angry with what the person has to say.

3. Check students' comprehension, using some or all of the following questions:

   a. Did Miss Henderson teach very well this morning?
   b. How did she teach?
   c. Why?
   d. Why was it a difficult experience for Miss Henderson?
   e. Why couldn't she do anything about it?

   f. Did Stuart type very well today?
   g. How did he type?
   h. Why?
   i. Why was it a difficult experience for Stuart?
   j. Why couldn't he do anything about it?

   k. Did the Johnson Brothers sing very well last night?
   l. How did they sing?
   m. Why?
   n. Why was it a difficult experience for the Johnson Brothers?
   o. Why couldn't they do anything about it?

p.   Did the President speak very well this afternoon?
q.   How did he speak?
r.   Why?
s.   Why was it a difficult experience for the President?
t.   Why couldn't he do anything about it?

CHECK-UP

Q & A

1.   Call on a pair of students to present the model.
2.   Have students work in pairs to create new dialogs.
3.   Call on pairs to present their new dialogs to the class.

Match

1.   f
2.   c
3.   h
4.   a
5.   b
6.   d
7.   e
8.   g

IN YOUR OWN WORDS

1.   Make sure students understand the instructions.
2.   Have students do the activity as written homework, using a dictionary for any new words they wish to use.
3.   Have students present and discuss what they have written, in pairs or as a class.

CHECK-UP

What's the Word?

I.   1.   Did   8.   Were
     2.   didn't   9.   wasn't
     3.   was   10.   was
     4.   were   11.   didn't
     5.   was   12.   Did
     6.   Did   13.   don't
     7.   did

II. 1. break
broke, he was playing

2. lose
lost, she was shopping

3. get
got, he was arguing

4. meet
met, she was working

5. cut
cut, he was slicing

6. burn
burned, I was baking

Listening

Have students complete the exercises as you play the tape or read the following:

Listen and chose the best answer.

1. Did you do well at your job interview yesterday? (a)
2. What did your children do this morning? (a)
3. What was she doing when she broke her arm? (b)
4. What was his supervisor doing? (b)
5. Sally, why did you fall asleep during class? (a)
6. Why didn't you finish your dinner? (b)

Text Pages 19–21: *Tell Me About Your Vacation*

FOCUS

> Review of the past tense:
> - More regular and irregular verbs
> - Information questions

INTRODUCING THE MODEL (Exercise 1)

1. Have students look at the model illustration.
2. Set the scene: "Mr. and Mrs. Blake are talking with some friends about their vacation."
3. Present the model.
4. Full-Class Choral Repetition.
5. Ask students if they have any questions; check understanding of vocabulary.
6. Group Choral Repetition.
7. Choral Conversation.
8. Call on one or two pairs of students to present the dialog.

   (For additional practice, do Choral Conversation in small groups or by rows.)

SIDE BY SIDE EXERCISES

Examples

> 2. A. Did you get there by boat?
>   B. No, we didn't.
>   A. How did you get there?
>   B. We got there by plane.
>
> 3. A. Did your plane leave on time?
>   B. No, it didn't.
>   A. How late did it leave?
>   B. It left two hours late.

1. **Exercise 2:** Introduce the new expressions *get there, by boat*. Review the verb *get–got*. Call on two students to present the dialog. Then do Choral Repetition and Choral Conversation Practice.
2. **Exercise 3:** Introduce the new expression *two hours late*. Review the verb *leave–left*. Same as above.
3. **Exercises 4–16:**

> **New vocabulary and verb review:**   4. *have–had, flight*   5. *stay–stayed*
>   6. *eat–ate*   7. *speak–spoke*   8. *take–took pictures*
>   9. *buy–bought, clothing, souvenir*   10. *swim–swam, Mediterranean, pool*
>   11. *see–saw, Colosseum, Vatican*   12. *travel–traveled around by taxi, by bus*
>   13. *send–sent, postcard*   14. *write–wrote, monument*
>   15. *meet–met, Italians, tourist*   16. *come–came, boat*

Culture Note

Exercise 11: Each year many people in Rome visit the Vatican, the seat of the Roman Catholic Church and home of the Pope. The Roman Colosseum, an ancient amphitheater, is a major tourist attraction in the city.

WORKBOOK

Pages 17–19

Exercise Note

Workbook p. 18: Students write about a vacation, using the pictures as a guide. Encourage students to use their imaginations and add any details they wish. Have students compare their stories.

ON YOUR OWN: *Trips and Travel*

Ask if any of your students have taken vacation trips or traveled from one place to another recently. If possible, have those students bring photographs or souvenirs to show the class. Encourage the other students in the class to participate by making comments and by asking questions such as those in the lesson.

Variation:

For homework, have students write about a vacation trip they took. Questions they should answer in their descriptions are:

Where did you go?   What did you see?
How did you get there?   What did you eat?
Where did you stay?   What did you buy?
                         How was your trip?

EXPANSION ACTIVITIES

1. *Role Play: I'm Sorry. I Can't Hear You!*

   In real life conversations, people often miss some of what they heard because of noise and distractions or a bad telephone connection. In this exercise, students practice asking for clarification about the part of the conversation they missed.

   a. Give students cards with statements on them such as the following:

      1. I went to (Rio de Janeiro) last week.
      2. My (father) just got back from France.
      3. When my family went to New York, our plane was (three) hours late.
      4. While we were visiting Rome, we ate in a lot of (fancy) restaurants.
      5. A friend of mine and I went to Africa by (boat) last summer.
      6. I remember when I went to the United States. The weather was (terrible).
      7. When I went to Germany, we spoke only (English).
      8. My family and I bought a lot of (clothing) in Paris two years ago.
      9. I really enjoyed my trip to the Mediterranean. We (swam) every day.
      10. The best thing about my trip to New York was that I saw the (Statue of Liberty).
      11. I'll never forget my trip to Canada because I lost my (suitcase).
      12. When I was in England, I traveled everywhere by (bicycle).
      13. I visited (Tokyo) last summer, and I loved it.
      14. We wanted to go to (Portugal) two years ago, but we just weren't able to.

b. Set the scene: "We're all at a party. We're talking about vacations and trips, but it's noisy and we can't always hear very well."

c. Have students who are holding cards choose another student to begin a conversation with. Have each student begin by reading the statement, but substituting the nonsense syllable *Bzzz* for the word in parentheses. For example:

A. I went to (*Bzzz*) last week.

Student B must answer "I'm sorry" and ask a question about the part of the communication he or she didn't understand. For example:

B. I'm sorry. WHERE did you go last week?

Student A repeats the statement, but this time he or she says the word in parentheses. The two students must then continue the dialog for two more lines, using any vocabulary they wish.

Example:

A. My *(Bzzz)* just got back from France.
B. I'm sorry. WHO just got back from France?
A. My *father* just got back from France.
B. Oh! That's nice. How long was he there?
A. He was there for a few weeks.

2. **What's the Question?**

a. Write the following sentence on the board:

> Mrs. Watson went to France last week.

b. Put a circle around different elements of the sentence and have students create a question based on that portion of the sentence. For example:

Teacher: (Mrs. Watson) went to France last week.
Student: Who went to France last week?

Teacher: Mrs. Watson went to France (last week.)
Student: When did Mrs. Watson go to France?

Teacher: Mrs. Watson went (to France) last week.
Student: Where did Mrs. Watson go last week?

Teacher: Mrs. Watson (went to France) last week.
Student: What did Mrs. Watson do last week?

c. Continue with other sentences. For example:

Teacher: Maria sells souvenirs (in Madrid) during the summer.
Student: Where does Maria sell souvenirs during the summer?

Teacher: Maria sells (souvenirs) in Madrid during the summer.
Student: What does Maria sell in Madrid during the summer?

Teacher: Maria sells souvenirs in Madrid (during the summer.)
Student: When does Maria sell souvenirs in Madrid?

Teacher: (Maria) sells souvenirs in Madrid during the summer.
Student: Who sells souvenirs in Madrid during the summer?

Page 10 A. A TERRIBLE NIGHTMARE

1. was	17. had
2. was	18. took
3. called	19. gave
4. got	20. stopped
5. drove	21. ate
6. reached	22. walked
7. got	23. arrived
8. was	24. looked
9. was	25. lost
10. started	26. decided
11. saw	27. was
12. looked	28. went
13. barked	29. shouted
14. saw	30. was
15. could	31. tripped
16. had	32. fell

Page 11 B. LISTEN

Listen and put a circle around the correct words.

1. We work.
2. We worked
3. Alan and John argued.
4. I shouted at my children
5. We visit our cousin.
6. We played football.
7. I ate a big breakfast.
8. Our neighbors sing.
9. We bake bread.
10. We drank coffee.
11. I had a bad headache
12. They walk home from work.
13. We studied English.
14. They practice the piano.
15. I wash the dishes.

Answers

1. every day	9. every week
2. yesterday evening	10. yesterday morning
3. yesterday	11. yesterday
4. yesterday evening	12. every day
5. every week	13. yesterday afternoon
6. last Friday	14. every evening
7. yesterday morning	15. every morning
8. every night	

Page 12 C. LISTEN

Listen and fill in the missing words. Then read the passage aloud.

My parents needed a lot of help when they moved to their new house. I lifted heavy furniture for them, and I painted all the rooms. When I visited one day, my mother said she wanted a garden. I waited until spring, and then I started one. I planted flowers and vegetables in the yard.

Yesterday my brother decided to move. I'm not complaining. I really like to help. But I think I'll be busy for a while!

Answers
1. needed
2. lifted
3. painted
4. visited
5. wanted
6. waited
7. started
8. planted
9. decided

Page 12 D. WHAT'S THE QUESTION?

1. Did you go
2. Did you buy
3. Did she forget
4. Did he teach
5. Did they come
6. Did she have
7. Did you see
8. Did he do
9. Did they steal
10. Did you lose

Page 13 E. SOMETHING DIFFERENT

1. didn't have, had
2. didn't sit, sat
3. didn't buy, bought
4. didn't sing, sang
5. didn't go, went
6. didn't drink, drank

7. didn't give, gave
8. didn't take, took
9. didn't get, got
10. didn't drive, drove
11. didn't ride, rode
12. didn't teach, taught

Page 14 F. WHAT ARE THEY SAYING?

1. Did you clean
   I didn't, was
2. Did you talk
   didn't
   wasn't
3. Did
   didn't, saw
4. Did
   didn't, was
   wrote
5. Did, ride
   didn't, was
6. Did
   I did, I read, was
7. DId
   she did, taught
   Were
   weren't
8. Did
   they did, were, ate
9. Did you
   did, I bought
   Did you buy
   weren't
10. Did you
    didn't, I hurt
    wasn't

Page 16 G. HOW DID IT HAPPEN?

1. She hurt herself while she was playing soccer.
2. He burned himself while he was ironing his clothes.
3. She cut herself while she was slicing onions.
4. She met him while she was fixing a flat tire.
5. He broke it while he was skating.
6. I lost it while I was riding my bicycle.
7. He met her while he was swimming at the beach.
8. He got it while he was fighting with his brother.

9. They burned themselves while they were making breakfast.
10. She tripped and fell while she was dancing.

Page 17 H. HOW DID IT HAPPEN?

1. Who did you visit?
2. What did you talk about?
3. Where did she go?
4. Who did she meet?
5. What did they speak?
6. Where did they swim?
7. When did he have dinner?
8. What kind of pie did you bake?
9. Why did she cry?
10. How long did you stay?
11. How did you come home?
12. How many hamburgers did he eat?
13. When did he leave the restaurant?
14. Why did they cover their eyes?
15. Who did she write a letter to?
16. How long did they study?
17. How many photographs did you take?
18. Who did you send a postcard to?
19. When did he fall asleep?
20. How/When did you lose your wallet?

Page 19 J. SOUND IT OUT

1. winter
2. interesting
3. movies
4. see
5. did
6. any
7. Linda
8. this
9. Did Linda see any interesting movies this winter?

10. tricks
11. three
12. magic
13. Irene
14. is
15. practicing
16. difficult
17. Irene is practicing three difficult magic tricks./ Is Irene practicing three difficult magic tricks?

CHAPTER 3 OVERVIEW: Text Pages 23–34

3

GRAMMAR

Future: Going to

What	am	I	going to do?
	is	he she it	
	are	we you they	

(I am)	I'm	going to read.
(He is)	He's	
(She is)	She's	
(It is)	It's	
(We are)	We're	
(You are)	You're	
(They are)	They're	

Possessive Pronouns

mine
his
hers
its
ours
yours
theirs

Future: Will

(I will)	I'll	work.
(He will)	He'll	
(She will)	She'll	
(It will)	It'll	
(We will)	We'll	
(You will)	You'll	
(They will)	They'll	

I He She It We You They	won't work.

Future Continuous Tense

(I will)	I'll	be working.
(He will)	He'll	
(She will)	She'll	
(It will)	It'll	
(We will)	We'll	
(You will)	You'll	
(They will)	They'll	

FUNCTIONS

Asking for and Reporting Information

Will *Richard get out of the hospital soon?*
Yes, *he* will.
No, *he* won't.

Will you *be home this evening?*
Yes, I will. I'll be *watching TV*
No, I won't. I'll be *working late at the office.*

Will *the movie* begin soon?
Will *the soup* be ready soon?
Will *Mom* be back soon?

How much longer will you be *studying English?*
I'll probably be *studying English* for another *30* minutes.

What are you looking forward to?
When is it going to happen?

What's the weather forecast?

Do you know anybody who *has a ladder?*

Tell me, *Doris,* _____?

Inquiring about Intention

What are you going to do?
What are you going to do *this weekend?*
What are you going to *plant?*

Are you going to *plant carrots this year?*

Expressing Intention

I'm going to *plant tomatoes.*

I'll *call you in 30 minutes.*
I'll *call him* right away.

Expressing Probability

I'll probably *be studying English for another 30 minutes.*

Requesting

Could you possibly do me a favor?
Could you do a favor for me?
Could I ask you a favor?

Could I possibly *borrow yours?*

Responding to Requests

Sure. What is it?

Greeting People

Hi, _____. This is
_____.

Can you talk for a minute?
I'm sorry. I can't talk right now.
I'm *studying English.* Can you call back a little later?

Leave Taking

Well, have a nice weekend.
You, too.

Speak to you soon.
Good-bye.

Apologizing

I'm sorry.

Expressing Inability

I'm sorry. I can't *talk right now.*

Expressing Obligation

I have to *fix my roof.*

Admitting

I'm afraid *I don't have one.*

Offering Advice

You should *call Charlie.*

Expressing Certainty

I'm sure *he'll be happy to lend you his.*

Expressing Gratitude

Thank you.

NEW VOCABULARY

a little later
a little while
a long time
call back
camping
Channel *2*
come back
composition
day off
emotional
Europe
European (adj)
fly (v)
football game
front door
give *the kids* a bath
go camping

Greece
hike (v)
ice skate (v)
imagine
income tax form
jack
jazz
last *January*
last *spring*
last *Sunday*
later
Latin American (adj)
mile
Mom
next *January*
next *spring*
next *Sunday*

perhaps
permanently
plan (n)
professor
relax
retirement
roof
say good-bye
screwdriver
semester
stay with
summer vacation
take *ballet* lessons
tap dance
this *January*
this *Monday night*
this *spring*

this *Sunday*
turkey
tuxedo
TV set
weather forecast
work late

as you can imagine
Could I ask you a favor?
Could you do a favor for me?
Could you possibly do me a favor?
Fine.
have a good life
Have a nice weekend.
have a party for
Speak to you soon.

LANGUAGE NOTES

1. **The Future Tense: Guidelines for Using *Going to* and *Will***

    a. In this chapter, *going to* is used to express a person's future plans or intentions. For example:

    > *Are you going to take ballet lessons this year?*
    > *No, I'm not. I'm going to take tap dance lessons.*
    >
    > *John is looking forward to this weekend.*
    > *He's going to relax at home with his family.*

    b. *Will* is used here to express a predictable or expected future event. For example:

    > *The play will begin at 8 o'clock.*
    > *The turkey won't be ready for several hours.*
    > *I'm sure he'll be happy to lend you his.*

    c. It is also common for *will* to be used when some sort of *qualification* is expressed:

    > I think I'll _____.
    > I'll probably _____.
    > Maybe I'll _____.
    > If _____, I'll _____.
    > I promise I'll _____.

2. **The Future Continuous Tense**

    This verb tense is commonly used to

    a. Emphasize the ongoing nature or duration of an activity in the future.

    > *How much longer will you be having dinner with your family?*
    > *I'll probably be having dinner for another thirty minutes.*

    b. Express a polite tone in talking about future events.

    > *I'll be taking you to see the other interesting tourist sights.*

Text Pages 24–25: *What Are They Going to Do?*

FOCUS

- Review of future: *going to*
- Contrast of the future tense and the past tense
- Contrast of future and past time expressions

GETTING READY

Review time expressions and contracted forms with *going to*.

1. Have students look at the list of time expressions on text page 24 as you read the examples below.

   > *George couldn't go shopping yesterday.*
   > *He's going to go shopping today.*

   > *Jane didn't study last night.*
   > *She's going to study tonight.*

   > *It isn't going to rain this week.*
   > *It's going to rain next week.*

2. Read the statements below and call on students to respond following the pattern above, using *going to* and a corresponding future time expression.

   a. Mr. and Mrs. Mason didn't come home from their vacation yesterday.
   b. Marylou couldn't clean her apartment last week.
   c. David can't write to his girlfriend this week.
   d. Shirley didn't take a trip last year.
   e. We didn't study very hard last month.
   f. Mr. Davis didn't visit his son last spring.
   g. Jim and Bob aren't going to study today.
   h. Mr. Brown didn't come to work last Monday.
   i. Gloria couldn't go skiing last January.
   j. The teachers didn't have a party yesterday.

INTRODUCING THE MODEL

1. Have students look at the model illustration.
2. Set the scene: "Two neighbors are talking about their vegetable gardens."
3. Present the model.
4. Full-Class Choral Repetition.
5. Ask students if they have any questions; check understanding of vocabulary.

   ### Language Note

   In informal speech, many speakers pronounce *going to* as *gonna*. Tell your students they will frequently hear this pronunciation.

6. Group Choral Repetition.
7. Choral Conversation.
8. Call on one or two pairs of students to present the dialog.

   (For additional practice, do Choral Conversation in small groups or by rows.)

SIDE BY SIDE EXERCISES

Examples

---

1. A. Is Ted going to wear his blue suit today?
   B. No, he isn't. He wore his blue suit yesterday.
   A. What's he going to wear?
   B. He's going to wear his black suit.

2. A. Is Barbara going to cook fish tonight?
   B. No, she isn't. She cooked fish last night.
   A. What's she going to cook?
   B. She's going to cook chicken.

---

1. **Exercise 1:** Review the irregular verb *wear–wore*. Call on one or two pairs of students to present the dialog. Then do Choral Repetition and Choral Conversation Practice.

2. **Exercise 2:** Same as above.

3. **Exercises 3–10:**

New vocabulary: 3. *Europe* 4. *jazz* 6. *Channel 2, this Monday night*
7. *professor, European, Latin American, semester* 8. *take ballet lessons, tap dance*
9. *grapes*

Language Note

Exercise 7: Titles such as *Professor* are capitalized when they are used as part of a person's name.

Culture Note

Exercise 4: Jazz is a type of music that sprang out of Afro-American spirituals, blues, and work songs and grew into a complex musical form. Many people feel that jazz is one of the most significant contributions to western culture that the United States has made.

Either Full-Class Practice or Pair Practice.

WORKBOOK

Pages 20–23 (Exercises A, B)

Exercise Notes

Workbook p. 22: For additional oral practice with Exercise B, have students act out the phone conversations.

Workbook p. 23: For additional oral practice with the forms of *will* in Exercise C, call on pairs of students to read the sentences aloud.

EXPANSION ACTIVITIES

1. **Role Play: *You Can't Be Serious!***

   a. Write on the board:

   > A. I'm going to _____ tomorrow.
   > B. { I don't believe it! / You can't be serious! } You just _____ last week
   > A. I know. But I'm going to _____ { again. / another _____. }
   > B. _____.
   > A. _____.

   b. Write some or all of these cues on the board or on word cards which you can give to students.

   1. buy a new _____
   2. go to a _____
   3. give my _____ a _____
       for _____ birthday
   4. drive to _____
   5. fly to _____
   6. take a _____ to _____
   7. paint my _____

   8. take _____ lessons
   9. visit _____
   10. go _____ing
   11. ride my bicycle to _____
   12. write a letter to _____
   13 complain to the landlord about _____
   14. read a book by _____
   15. knit a _____

   c. Have pairs of students create dialogs based on the model on the board. Encourage students to expand the conversation in any way they wish. For example:

   > A. I'm going to buy a new coat tomorrow.
   > B. You can't be serious! You just bought a new coat last week!
   > A. I know. But I'm going to buy another coat.
   >
   >   (Possible expansion)
   >
   > B. Why are you going to do that?
   > A. Because I need two coats this winter.

   > A. I'm going to fly to Rio tomorrow.
   > B. I don't believe it! You just flew to Rio last week!
   > A. I know. But I'm going to fly to Rio again.
   >
   >   (Possible expansion)
   >
   > B. What are you going to do there?
   > A. I'm going to meet a friend and travel around the country.

2. ***Classroom Interviews***

   a. Write the following times on the board:

   > after class
   > tonight
   > this weekend

   b. On a separate piece of paper, have students write three sentences about plans they have, using the time expressions on the board. For example:

   > I'm going to have lunch after class.
   > I'm going to watch TV tonight.
   > I'm going to see a movie this weekend.

c. Collect the papers and distribute them randomly to different students in the class.

d. Have each student interview others (for example: "What are you going to do tonight?" "Are you going to see a movie this weekend?") in order to find out whose plans match those on his or her particular card.

e. Once everybody has identified the correct person, call on students to tell about the person on their card. For example:

> "Thomas is going to go home after class.
> He's going to study tonight.
> He's going to visit his cousins this weekend."

READING: *Plans for the Weekend*

FOCUS

Future: *going to*

NEW VOCABULARY

go camping   weather forecast
plan (n)

PREVIEWING THE STORY (optional)

Have students talk about the story title and/or illustration. Introduce new vocabulary.

READING THE STORY

1. Have students read silently, or follow along silently as the story is read aloud by you, by one or more students, or on the tape.
2. Ask students if they have any questions; check understanding of vocabulary.

   Language Note

   To rain cats and dogs means to rain very hard.

3. Check students' comprehension, using some or all of the following questions:

   a. What's Doris going to do this weekend?
   b. What's Michael going to do?
   c. What are Tom and Jane going to do?
   d. What's Peter going to do?
   e. What's Rita going to do?
   f. What are Karen and her friends going to do?
   g. Why are they all going to be disappointed?

CHECK-UP

Q & A

1. Call on a pair of students to present the model.
2. Have students work in pairs to create new dialogs.
3. Call on pairs to present their new dialogs to the class.

HOW ABOUT YOU?

Have students answer the questions in pairs or as a class.

Listening

Have students answer the exercises as you play the tape or read the following:

Listen to the conversation and choose the answer that is true.

1. A. Don't wear your blue suit tonight. You wore it last weekend.
   B. All right. Where's my BLACK suit?   (b)

2. A. Do we need anything from the supermarket?
   B. Yes. We need some beef, some potatoes, and some tomatoes.   (b)

3. A. Which movie do you want to see?
   B. How about "The Man in the Brown Suit"?
   A. Okay. What channel is it on?   (b)

4. A. What are you going to do tomorrow?
   B. I'm going to plant lettuce, tomatoes, and beans.   (b)

5. A. What's the matter with it?
   B. The brakes don't work, and it doesn't start very well in the morning.   (a)

6. A. This car is very nice, but it's too expensive.
   B. You're right.   (b)

Text Page 27: *Will Richard Get Out of the Hospital Soon?*

FOCUS

> Review of the future tense with *will*

GETTING READY

Review *will* and *won't*.

1. Write on the board:

    > Yes, _____ will.
    > No, _____ won't. (_____'ll _____.)

2. Ask *yes/no* questions about some predictable future event in your students' lives. Have students respond, using any of the forms on the board. For example:

    "Will we finish class at (12 o'clock)?"   "Will you come to school (next Tuesday)?"
    "Yes, we will."   "No, I won't. I'll come to school (next Wednesday)."

    "Will class start at (9 o'clock) tomorrow?"
    "No, it won't. It'll start at (10 o'clock)."

INTRODUCING THE MODEL

There are two model conversations. Introduce and practice each separately. For each model:

1. Have students look at the model illustration.
2. Set the scene:

    1st model: "Two people are talking about Richard."
    2nd model: "Two people are talking about Sherman."

3. Present the model.
4. Full-Class Choral Repetition.
5. Ask students if they have any questions; check understanding of vocabulary.
6. Group Choral Repetition.
7. Choral Conversation.
8. Call on one or two pairs of students to present the dialog.

    (For additional practice, do Choral Conversation in small groups or by rows.)

SIDE BY SIDE EXERCISES

Examples

> 1. A. Will the movie begin soon?   2. A. Will the game begin soon?
>   B. Yes, it will. It'll begin at 8:00.   B. No, it won't. It won't begin until 3:00.

1. **Exercise 1:** Call on two students to present the dialog. Then do Choral Repetition and Choral Conversation Practice.
2. **Exercise 2:** Same as above.
3. **Exercises 3–8:**

> **New vocabulary:** 6. *turkey* 7. *Mom, a little while* 8. *a long time*

Language Note

Exercise 7: There are many informal ways to address one's mother and father. For example:

Mother: *Mom, Mommy, Momma, Mama, Ma, Mum, Mummy*
Father: *Daddy, Dad, Pa, Papa, Pop, Poppa*

Culture Note

Exercise 8: A sign with the words *Just Married* is sometimes on the car of a newly married couple as they leave for their honeymoon.

Either Full-Class Practice or Pair Practice.

WORKBOOK

Pages 23–24 (Exercise C)

EXPANSION ACTIVITY

Telephone Role Play: At the Office

1. Write on the board:

> A. Hello, _____. May I help you?
> B. Yes. Could I please speak to _____?
> A. I'm sorry. _____ isn't in the office right now. Would you like to leave a message for _____?
> B. No, thank you. That won't be necessary. When do you think _____'ll be back?
> A. { _____ probably won't be back (for/until) _____.
>   { _____'ll probably be back in about _____. }
> B. Thank you very much. I'll call back later.
> A. You're welcome. Good-bye.

2. Divide the class into pairs and have students role play this telephone conversation. Have students use any names and time expressions they wish. Give Speaker A in each pair a card showing the name of a business, such as those below. Encourage students to make up other names of businesses if they wish.

Carlson Computer Company	Smith Tire Company
Gold Star Travel Company	Sure Technology Company
Rock Village Apartments	Jones Law Associates
Real Engineering Company	True Insurance Company
Big Boy Paper Company	Goodman's Department Store
Wilson Trucking, Incorporated	Presto Furniture Company
Dr. Peterson's Office	Larson Auto Supply

3. Call on a few pairs of students to present their role plays to the class without referring to the model on the board. For example:

    A. Hello, Carlson Computer Company. May I help you?
    B. Yes. Could I please speak to Ms. Blake?
    A. I'm sorry. She isn't in the office right now. Would you like to leave a message for her?
    B. No, thank you. That won't be necessary. When do you think she'll be back?
    A. She'll probably be back in about thirty minutes.
    B. Thank you very much. I'll call back later.
    A. You're welcome. Good-bye.

Text Page 28: *Will You Be Home This Evening?*

FOCUS

> Review of the future continuous tense

GETTING READY

Review the future continuous tense.

1. Write on the board:

Mr. Davis	Spanish
Mrs. Davis	Arabic
Betty and Fred Davis	Russian
Martha Davis	Swedish
Bob Davis	German

2. Set the scene: "Everyone in the Davis family loves languages. This year they'll all be studying new languages. For example, Mr. Davis will be studying Spanish."
3. Have students ask and answer about the others, using the future continuous tense. For example:

   A. What will Mrs. Davis be studying?
   B. She'll be studying Arabic.

INTRODUCING THE MODEL

There are two model conversations. Introduce and practice each separately. For each model:

1. Have students look at the model illustration in the book.
2. Set the scene:

   1st model: "Two friends are talking."
   2nd model: "Two people are talking about Jane."

3. Present the model.
4. Full-Class Choral Repetition.
5. Ask students if they have any questions; check understanding of vocabulary.
6. Group Choral Repetition.
7. Choral Conversation.
8. Call on one or two pairs of students to present the dialog.

   (For additional practice, do Choral Conversation in small groups or by rows.)

SIDE BY SIDE EXERCISES

Examples

> 1. A. Will Tom be home this evening?
>   B. Yes, he will. He'll be reading.
>
> 2. A. Will Mr. and Mrs. Harris be home this evening?
>   B. Yes, they will. They'll be painting their bathroom.
>
> 3. A. Will you be home this evening?
>   B. No, I won't. I'll be swimming.

1. **Exercise 1:** Call on two students to present the dialog. Then do Choral Repetition and Choral Conversation Practice.

2. **Exercise 2:** Same as above.

3. **Exercises 3–9:**

> **New vocabulary:**   5. *ice skate*   8. *income tax form*

Culture Note

Exercise 8: Federal income taxes in the United States are due on April 15th of every year. Many people fill out the forms themselves, while others hire an accountant to fill out these forms for them.

Either Full-Class Practice or Pair Practice.

WORKBOOK

Page 25

EXPANSION ACTIVITIES

1. *What Will They Be Doing?*

   a. Have the class listen as you tell about people who are getting new jobs or changing jobs.

   b. Then call on several students to tell what the person will be doing in his or her new job. Whenever possible, hold up a visual for the occupation as you talk about it. (You can use *Side by Side* Picture Cards 94–120.) For example:

   > "Mary will start her new job as an English teacher next week."

   Possible responses:

   > "She'll be going to school every day."
   > "She'll be teaching English."
   > "She'll be speaking English to students."

Other ways to introduce the situations:

1. Joe just got a new job as a (truck driver). He'll start the job next month.
2. A company just hired Marie as a (secretary). She'll start work next Monday.
3. John studied (cooking) for several years. A very good (restaurant) just hired him to be the (chef).
4. David just got a job as (an auto mechanic).
5. Susan is a (plumber). She'll start her first job soon.

2. *Writing Predictions: Five Years from Now*

a. Write on the board:

I'll be _____ing.
I won't be _____ing.

b. On a separate piece of paper, have each student use the patterns on the board to write a short prediction of what he or she will be doing five years from now. For example:

Five years from now, I'll be living in Mexico City. I won't be studying English any more. I'll be working for a large import-export company.

c. Collect the papers and read them aloud. Have the class guess which student wrote each prediction.

Text Page 29: *Can You Call Back a Little Later?*

FOCUS

Review of the future continuous tense

INTRODUCING THE MODEL

1. Have students look at the model illustration.
2. Set the scene: "Two friends are talking on the telephone."
3. Present the model.
4. Full-Class Choral Repetition.
5. Ask students if they have any questions; check understanding of new vocabulary: *call back, a little later, speak to you soon.*
6. Group Choral Repetition.
7. Choral Conversation.
8. Call on one or two pairs of students to present the dialog.

   (For additional practice, do Choral Conversation in small groups or by rows.)

SIDE BY SIDE EXERCISES

Examples

1. A. Hi, (Bob). This is (Harry). Can you talk for a minute?
   B. I'm sorry. I can't talk right now. I'm studying English. Can you call back a little later?
   A. Sure. How much longer will you be studying English?
   B. I'll probably be studying English for another (twenty) minutes.
   A. Fine. I'll call you in (twenty) minutes.
   B. Speak to you soon.
   A. Good-bye.

2. A. Hi, (Linda). This is (Jane). Can you talk for a minute?
   B. I'm sorry. I can't talk right now. I'm helping my children with their homework. Can you call back a little later?
   A. Sure. How much longer will you be helping your children with their homework?
   B. I'll probably be helping my children with their homework for another (forty-five) minutes.
   A Fine. I'll call you in (forty-five) minutes.
   B. Speak to you soon.
   A. Good-bye.

1. **Exercise 1:** Call on two students to present the dialog. Then do Choral Repetition and Choral Conversation Practice.
2. **Exercise 2:** Same as above.
3. **Exercises 3–5:**

New vocabulary: 5. *give the kids a bath*

Either Full-Class Practice or Pair Practice.

4. **Exercise 6:** Have students use the model as a guide to create their own conversations, using vocabulary of their choice. Encourage students to use dictionaries to find new words they want to use. This exercise can be done orally in class or for written homework. If you assign it for homework, you should do one example in class to make sure students understand what's expected. Have students present their conversations in class the next day.

WORKBOOK

Page 26

Exercise Note

Workbook p. 26: This exercise reviews the future continuous tense while allowing students to fill in the blanks with any places in their city they wish. Call on students to present their *tours* to the class.

EXPANSION ACTIVITIES

1. **Telephone Role Plays**

   a. Write situations such as those below on word cards. Each situation involves talking on the telephone.

   b. Divide the class into pairs and give each pair a situation. (You can give the same situation to more than one pair.) Have the students prepare 4–8 line telephone dialogs based on the situations.

   c. Have each pair read their situation and then present their dialog to the class. Use props such as telephones to make the dialogs more realistic.

   Situations:

   1. A person is talking to a mechanic on the phone. The mechanic is fixing his/her car, but it isn't ready.

   2. Someone is calling a friend. The mother answers the phone. The friend is painting his/her room and can't come to the phone.

   3. A secretary is going to be late for work because he/she has a flat tire. The secretary has to call the boss to say he/she is going to be late.

   4. Jimmy can't go to his music lesson this afternoon because he's sick. Jimmy's mother or father has to call the music teacher.

   5. A husband and wife are talking on the phone. It's already late, and one of them is still working at the office.

   6. One of you has a doctor's appointment tomorrow. You won't be able to go. Call the doctor's office to tell them.

2. **Students Talk about Themselves**

   Have students talk about scheduled future events in their own lives. For example, ask:

   > "What will you be doing next summer?"
   > "What will you be studying next semester?"

3. **Celebrity Travel Plans**

   a. Divide the class into small groups.

   b. Give each group a card with the name of a famous person. For example:

| the President | the Prime Minister | (name of a famous movie star) |

| (name of a famous singer) | (name of a famous sports star) |

c. Write the following on the board:

> I'll be _____ing.
>
> leave _____ for _____
> meet with _____
> go to _____
> visit _____
> talk to _____
> have lunch/dinner with _____
> return to _____

d. Have each group work together, choosing expressions from the board, to write imaginary travel plans for the person on their card.

e. When the groups have finished, call on one person to read each group's itinerary and have the other students in the class try to guess who the famous person is. For example:

> "Tonight I'll be leaving Washington for Miami. Tomorrow morning I'll be meeting with local politicians. In the afternoon, I'll be talking to the mayor about problems of the city. Then, I'll be returning to Washington. Who am I?"

Text Page 30

READING: *Saying Good-bye*

FOCUS

- Future: *will*
- Future continuous tense

NEW VOCABULARY

as you can imagine	have a good life
come back	perhaps
emotional	permanently
fly (v)	say good-bye
for a long time	stay with

PREVIEWING THE STORY (optional)

Have students talk about the story title and/or illustrations. Introduce new vocabulary.

READING THE STORY

1. Have students read silently, or follow along silently as the story is read aloud by you, by one or more students, or on the tape.
2. Ask students if they have any questions; check understanding of vocabulary.
3. Check students' comprehension, using some or all of the following questions:

   a. Where are Mr. and Mrs. Anastas?
   b. What are they doing?
   c. What will Dimitri and his family do in a few minutes?
   d. Why won't Mr. and Mrs. Anastas be seeing them for a long time?
   e. Where are Dimitri and his family going to live?
   f. Who are they going to stay with?
   g. What will Dimitri do?
   h. What will his wife, Anna, do?
   i. What will their children do?
   j. Why are Mr. and Mrs. Anastas happy?
   k. Why are Mr. and Mrs. Anastas sad?
   l. Why are they going to be lonely?
   m. What will they do some day?

CHECK-UP

True or False?

1. False
2. True
3. False
4. True
5. False

IN YOUR OWN WORDS

1. Make sure students understand the instructions.
2. Have students do the activity as written homework, using a dictionary for any new words they wish to use.
3. Have students present and discuss what they have written, in pairs or as a class.

Text Pages 31–32: *Could You Possibly Do Me a Favor?*

FOCUS

> • Review of possessive pronouns
> • Review of *should* to give advice
> • Introduction of *could* to make requests

GETTING READY

Review possessive pronouns.

1. Write on the board:

2. Read each statement below and point to one of the three illustrations on the board. Have students make a similar statement about the person or people you are pointing to, using the possessive pronoun. For example:

> You: "I lost my wallet."
> (point to Doris)
> Students: "Doris lost hers, too."

a. I lost my book.
b. I lost my cat.
c. I did well on my examination.
d. I like my job.
e. I like my friends.
f. I sold my bicycle.

g. I called my boss.
h. I want to sell my books.
i. My teacher is wonderful.
j. My classes are interesting.
k. My stove is broken.

INTRODUCING THE MODEL

1. Have students look at the model illustration.
2. Set the scene: "Two neighbors are talking. One of them is asking a favor."
3. Present the model.
4. Full-Class Choral Repetition.
5. Ask students if they have any questions; check understanding of new vocabulary and expressions:

> *Could you possibly do me a favor? Could you do a favor for me? Could I ask you a favor?*

6. Group Choral Repetition.
7. Choral Conversation.
8. Call on one or two pairs of students to present the dialog.

(For additional practice, do Choral Conversation in small groups or by rows.)

SIDE BY SIDE EXERCISES

Examples

1. A. Could you possibly do me a favor?*
   B. Sure. What is it?
   A. I've got a problem. I have to fix my TV set, and I don't have a screwdriver. Could I possibly borrow YOURS?
   B. I'm sorry. I'm afraid I don't have one.
   A. Oh. Do you know anybody who DOES?
   B. Yes. You should call Jane. I'm sure she'll be happy to lend you hers.
   A. Thank you. I'll call her right away.

2. A. Could you possibly do me a favor?*
   B. Sure. What is it?
   A. I've got a problem. I have to fix my front door, and I don't have a hammer. Could I possibly borrow YOURS?
   B. I'm sorry. I'm afraid I don't have one.
   A. Oh. Do you know anybody who DOES?
   B. Yes. You should call Paul. I'm sure he'll be happy to lend you his.
   A. Thank you. I'll call him right away.

*Or: Could you do a favor for me?   Could I ask you a favor?

1. **Exercise 1:** Introduce the new words *TV set, screwdriver.* Call on two students to present the dialog. Then do Choral Repetition and Choral Conversation Practice.

2. **Exercise 2:** Introduce the new words *front door, hammer.* Same as above.

3. **Exercises 3–5:**

> **New vocabulary:**   3. *composition*   4. *jack*   5. *tuxedo*

Either Full-Class Practice or Pair Practice.

4. **Exercise 6:** Have students use the model as a guide to create their own conversations, using vocabulary of their choice. Encourage students to use dictionaries to find new words they want to use. This exercise can be done orally in class or for written homework. If you assign it for homework, you should do one example in class to make sure students understand what's expected. Have students present their conversations in class the next day.

WORKBOOK

Page 27

EXPANSION ACTIVITIES

1. Write and Present a Dialog

a. Write on the board:

> A. Could you possibly _____
> _____?
> B. I'm really sorry, but I can't because _____
> _____
> _____.

b. Divide the class into pairs and have each pair write a dialog based on the model. Students can write about any type of request or favor and give any reason for refusing.

c. Have students present their dialogs to the class. For example:

A. Could you possibly drive me to the airport this afternoon? I have to take a plane to Chicago, and my car is at the repair shop.
B. I'm really sorry, but I can't because I have to go to my English class at 3 o'clock.
A. Don't worry about it. I'll ask somebody else.

A. Could you possibly take a few packages to the post office for me? I have to take my son to the doctor's office, and I'm already late for the appointment.
B. I'm really sorry, but I can't because I have to stay home and wait for the plumber. Maybe Jane can take your packages to the post office. Why don't you call her?

2. Role Play: Could I Ask You a Favor?

a. Divide the class into pairs.

b. Write the following situations on index cards. Give Role A to one member of the pair and Role B to the other.

c. Have students practice their role plays and then present them to the class.

1.

Role A:	Role B:
Your car is broken, and you need a ride to work today. Ask your friend.	You aren't going to work today because you have a very bad cold.

2.

Role A:	Role B:
Your bicycle has a flat tire, and you can't find your jack. Ask your friend.	Your sister borrowed your jack last week, and she forgot to return it.

3.

Role A:	Role B:
You're baking a cake, and you just realized you don't have any more flour! Your next-door neighbor is walking out of the building. Maybe your neighbor is going to the supermarket.	You're walking out of your apartment building. First, you're going to the bank. Then, you're going to the post office. After that, you're going to the drug store. And finally, you're going to the supermarket.

ON YOUR OWN: *Looking Forward*

FOCUS

> Review of *going to*

ON YOUR OWN ACTIVITY

For each situation:

1. Have students look at the illustration and cover the text as you read or play the tape.
2. Then have students look at the text and follow along as you read or play the tape again.
3. Ask students if they have any questions; check understanding of new vocabulary:

> 1. *looking forward to, magazines, relax*   2. *have a party for*
> 3. *hike, mile,*   4. *retirement*

4. Ask questions about the situation and/or have students ask each other questions. For example:

   1. What's John looking forward to?
      Is he going to think about work all weekend?
      What's he going to do?

   2. What's Alice looking forward to?
      Why?
      Who's going to be at the party?

   3. What are Mr. and Mrs. Williams looking forward to?
      Where are they going to go?
      What are they going to do there?

   4. What's George looking forward to?
      Why?

5. Have students talk about what they are looking forward to. Divide students into pairs. Have each student find out about something the other is looking forward to and then report back to the class. For example:

   "Barbara is looking forward to this weekend because she's going to go to her sister's wedding. She's looking forward to it because everybody in her family is going to be there."

   "Richard is looking forward to his winter vacation because he's going to go skiing during the day and sit in front of a warm fireplace every evening."

Variation:

For homework, have students write about something they're looking forward to.

WORKBOOK

Pages 28–30 (Exercises G, H)

Check-Up Test: Pages 30–32

Page 20   A.   WHAT ARE THEY SAYING?

1. No, we didn't, gave
   We're going to give
2. No, she didn't
   went, She's going to go
3. No, I didn't, wrote
   I'm going to write
4. No, they didn't, drove
   They're going to drive
5. No, I didn't, wore
   I'm going to wear
6. No, we didn't, read
   We're going to read
7. No, he didn't, sent
   He's going to send
8. No, I didn't, left
   I'm going to leave
9. No, I didn't
   did
   I'm going to do
10. No, we didn't
    ate
    We're going to eat
11. No, I didn't, saw
    I'm going to see
12. No, they didn't, spoke
    They're going to speak

Page 22   B.   BAD CONNECTIONS

1. your doctor going to do
2. are you going to go
3. is his best friend going to move
4. What are your parents going to give you?
5. Who is your daughter going to go out with?
6. When are you going to get married?
7. Who are you going to visit?
8. What are Peggy and John going to name their new baby?
9. Why are you going to fire me?
10. Where are we going to go?

Page 23   C.   I'M AFRAID

1. won't have	1. you will
	you'll

2. will catch
3. won't start
4. will forget
5. won't fix
6. won't be
7. will have
8. won't lose
9. won't like
10. will be

2. she won't
   She won't
3. it will
   it'll
4. they won't
   they won't
5. he will
   he'll
6. you will
   You'll
7. he won't
   he won't
8. you will
   you'll
9. she will
   She'll
10. they won't
    They won't

Page 25   D.   EVERYBODY'S BUSY

1. she will
   She'll be studying
2. I will, I'll be
   practicing the violin
3. they will
   They'll be playing
   tennis
4. she will, She'll
   be fixing her car
5. he will, He'll be
   cleaning his garage
6. he will, He'll be
   washing clothes
7. she will, She'll be
   planting flowers
8. we will, We'll be
   dancing

Page 27   F.   DID YOU HEAR?

1. yours
2. ours
3. His
4. His
5. hers
6. Hers
7. theirs
8. theirs
9. yours
10. mine
11. mine

Page 28 G. WHAT DOES IT MEAN?

1. a	9. b
2. b	10. b
3. b	11. c
4. b	12. c
5. a	13. a
6. b	14. b
7. a	15. c
8. c	

Page 30 H. LISTEN: *Looking Forward*

Listen and answer the questions after each story.

What's Henry Looking Forward to?

Henry is looking forward to this summer. He and his family are going to move from New York City to a little town in California. They aren't going to live in an apartment again. They're going to live in a house with a yard. And after they move into their new house, they're going to get a dog.

1. Why are Henry and his family looking forward to this summer?
2. Are they going to live in an apartment or a house?
3. What are they going to do after they move?

What's Bobby Looking Forward to?

Bobby is happy because his mother is going to come home from the hospital this afternoon. Last week she was very sick, and she had to have an operation. But the doctor says she's going to be just fine. When she comes home, Bobby's mother will have to stay in bed for a few weeks. After that, she'll be able to go back to work.

1. Why is Bobby happy?
2. Why was Bobby's mother in the hospital?
3. What will she have to do when she gets home?
4. After that, what will she be able to do?

What's Julie Looking Forward to?

Here I am! I'm sitting at my desk in my office, but I'm not working. I'm thinking about my vacation. Just think! In two weeks I'll be camping in the mountains. I won't be sitting at my desk, and I won't be typing. I'll be swimming and hiking during the day. And I'll be reading some good books and going to bed early every evening. I'm really excited about my vacation!

1. Where's Julie?
2. What's she doing?
3. What will she be doing during the day on her vacation?

4. What will she be doing every evening?
5. What *won't* she be doing?

Answers

What's Henry Looking Forward to?

1. They're going to move from New York City to a little town in California.
2. They're going to live in a house.
3. They're going to get a dog.

What's Bobby Looking Forward to?

1. His mother is going to come home from the hospital this afternoon.
2. She was very sick, and she had to have an operation.
3. She'll have to stay in bed for a few weeks.
4. She'll be able to go back to work.

What's Julie Looking Forward to?

1. She's sitting at her desk in her office.
2. She's thinking about her vacation.
3. She'll be swimming and hiking.
4. She'll be reading some good books and going to bed early.
5. She won't be sitting at her desk, and she won't be typing.

CHECK-UP TEST: *CHAPTERS 1–3*

Page 30 A.

1. are	3. you're
swim	skater
2. drives	4. aren't
She's	players, play

Page 31 B.

1. didn't, was	4. Did,
wrote	didn't, spoke
2. were	wasn't
didn't	5. Did
bought	did, was
3. Did	ate
didn't	6. get
taught	didn't
was	were

Page 31 C.

1. What are you writing about?
2. Who are they going to call?
3. Where did she swim?

4. When will he be ready?
5. How did they come?
6. How many photographs is she going to take?
7. How long will you be staying in London?

Page 32   D.

1. She's visiting her neighbors.
2. He watches TV.
3. We're having a party.
4. They went bowling.
5. He was baking bread.
6. I'm going to clean my apartment.
7. We'll be playing cards.
8. She'll take the bus.

Page 32   E.

Listen to each question and then complete the answer.

Ex. Does Betty like to swim?

1. Is your brother a good typist?
2. Will Mary be here soon?
3. Does Mr. Smith dance well?
4. Did your children visit you yesterday?
5. Are your students doing their homework?
6. Does Jane have to go home?
7. Will you and Edward be cooking tonight?
8. Did Mrs. Roberts live on Main Street last year?

Answers

1. he is
2. she will
3. he doesn't
4. they did
5. they aren't
6. she does
7. we won't
8. she didn't

GRAMMAR

Present Perfect Tense

(I have)	I've			I			
(We have)	We've			We	haven't		
(You have)	You've			You			
(Thoy havo)	Thoy'vo	eaten.		Thoy		eaten.	
(He has)	He's			He			
(She has)	She's			She	hasn't		
(It has)	It's			It			

Have	I we you they	eaten?		Yes,	I we you they	have.		No,	I we you they	haven't.
Has	he she it				he she it	has.			he she it	hasn't.

Irregular Verbs

do – did – done	see – saw – seen	buy – bought – bought	read – read – read
drink – drank – drunk	speak – spoke – spoken	feed – fed – fed	say – said – said
eat – ate – eaten	swim – swam – swum	feel – felt – felt	spend – spent – spent
get – got – gotten	take – took – taken	leave – left – left	
give – gave – given	wear – wore – worn	make – made – made	
go – went – gone	write – wrote – written	meet – met – met	
ride – rode – ridden		pay – paid – paid	

FUNCTIONS

Asking for and Reporting Information

I've already *given blood this week.*
Really? When?
I *gave blood yesterday.*

I haven't *swum* in a long time.
Why not?
I just haven't had the time.

Have you *seen the new Walt Disney movie* yet?
Yes, I have. I *saw it yesterday.*

Has *Peter left for work* yet?
No, *he* hasn't.

I still haven't *typed two important letters.*

Have you *seen any good movies* recently?
Yes, I have. I *saw a very good movie just last week.*
What *movie* did you *see*?
I *saw The Return of Superman.*

Inquiring about Intention

Are you going to *give blood today*?
What are you going to do *tonight*?
What *movie* are you going to *see*?

Expressing Uncertainty

I'm not sure.
I don't know.

Expressing Want-Desire

I really want to *see a good movie.*

Inquiring about Likes/Dislikes

Do you like to *swim*?
And you liked it?

Expressing Likes

I LOVED it!

Expressing Obligation

I have to *finish it now.*
He has to *leave now.*

Expressing an Opinion

I think *it's* one of the best *movies* I've ever *seen.*

Initiating a Conversation

I see *you haven't gone home yet.*

Expressing Agreement

That's right.

Leave Taking

Have a good weekend.
You, too.

NEW VOCABULARY

already	office clerk
aspirin	on *my* way to
at this point	paycheck
beginning (n)	play cards
best friend	recently
Bingo	surprised
bookkeeper	take a test
co-worker	take a tour
desk	take *her* medicine
do *her* food shopping	top
driver's test	tour (n)
Empire State Building	typical
extremely	United Nations
get rid of	Walt Disney movie
give blood	World Trade Center
go bowling	yet
go dancing	
have the time	as for me
health club	do a lot of things
mail room	Have a good weekend.
make plans for	I see . . .
medicine	Look
Monopoly	That's right.
New York Times	Well, . . .

Verbs		
bake	baked	baked
buy	bought	bought
call	called	called
do	did	done
eat	ate	eaten
feed	fed	fed
finish	finished	finished
get	got	gotten
give	gave	given
go	went	gone
leave	left	left
make	made	made
meet	met	met
pay	paid	paid
read	read	read
ride	rode	ridden
say	said	said
see	saw	seen
speak	spoke	spoken
spend	spent	spent
swim	swam	swum
take	took	taken
wash	washed	washed
wear	wore	worn
write	wrote	written

LANGUAGE NOTES

Present Perfect Tense

1. The present perfect tense is formed with *have/has* plus the past participle form of the verb. (*Have/has* is usually contracted in informal language.)

2. The past participle of most verbs is the same as the past tense form. For example:

    (walk–walked–walked)   I walked to school yesterday.
    I've walked to school every day this week.

    (buy–bought–bought)   She bought a book this morning.
    She's bought several books recently.

    Some verbs have a different past participle form. For example:

    (go–went–gone)   We went to a concert last night.
    We've gone to several concerts this year.

    In this chapter, past participles that are not the same as the past tense form are given in the lessons. Students can also refer to the verb list in the Appendix at the back of the student text.

3. Verbs in the present perfect tense are associated with a period of time beginning in the past and continuing up to the present. This tense differs from the past, which may be used to refer to a specific point in time. Compare:

    I haven't seen a good movie in a long time.
    I saw a very good movie last month.

4. In this chapter, the present perfect is introduced with several time expressions commonly used with this tense: *in a long time, already, yet, recently, ever.*

5. Because the present perfect tense is associated with an indefinite period of time, it is often used to open topics of conversation. For example:

    Have you seen the new Walt Disney movie yet?
    Have you read any good books recently?

Text Pages 36–37: *They've Already Seen a Movie This Week*

FOCUS

Introduction of the present perfect tense:
- Affirmative statements
- Expressions with *already*

INTRODUCING THE MODEL

1. Have students look at the model illustration.
2. Set the scene: "Two people are talking about Mr. and Mrs. Smith."
3. Present the model.
4. Full-Class Choral Repetition.
5. Ask students if they have any questions; check understanding of new vocabulary: *They've already seen.*
6. Group Choral Repetition.
7. Choral Conversation.
8. Call on one or two pairs of students to present the dialog.

   (For additional practice, do Choral Conversation in small groups or by rows.)

9. Use the sentence *They've already seen a movie this week* to introduce the other forms of the present perfect tense.

   a. Point to yourself and say, "I've already seen a movie this week." Have students repeat chorally and individually.

   b. Continue in the same way for the other pronouns. For example:

      "We've already seen a movie this week."

   Have students refer to the box at the top of the page. Check pronunciation of contractions with *have* and provide additional practice if necessary.

10. Call on several pairs of students to practice the model, using other names/pronouns in place of *Mr. and Mrs. Smith.* For example:

    (you)
    A. Are you going to see a movie tonight?
    B. No, I'm not. I've already seen a movie this week.
    A. Really? When?
    B. I saw a movie yesterday.

SIDE BY SIDE EXERCISES

Examples

1. A. Are Mr. and Mrs. Smith going to eat at a restaurant tonight?
   B. No, they aren't. They've already eaten at a restaurant this week.
   A. Really? When?
   B. They ate at a restaurant yesterday.

2. A. Is Frank going to get a haircut today?
   B. No, he isn't. He's already gotten a haircut this week.
   A. Really? When?
   B. He got a haircut yesterday.

1. **Exercise 1:** Introduce the past participle of the verb *eat: eat–ate–eaten.* Call on two students to present the dialog. Then do Choral Repetition and Choral Conversation Practice.

2. **Exercise 2:** Introduce the past participle of the verb *get: get–got–gotten;* introduce the new expression *get a haircut.* Same as above.

3. **Exercises 3–10:** The verbs in these exercises have irregular past participles; they are not the same as the past tense form.

> **New vocabulary and past participles:** 3. *written* 4. *taken* 5. *give blood, given* 6. *seen*
> 7. *gone* 8. *worn* 9. *do her food shopping, done* 10. *swum, health club*

Introduce the past participle of each verb and any new vocabulary before doing each exercise. Either Full-Class Practice or Pair Practice.

4. **Exercises 11–14:** The verbs in these exercises have regular past participles; they are the same as the past tense form.

> **New vocabulary and past participles:** 11. *washed* 12. *Bingo, played* 13. *bought*
> 14. *spent*

Introduce the past participle of each verb before doing each exercise. Either Full-Class Practice or Pair Practice.

Culture Note

Exercise 12: Bingo is a popular game. Numbers are called out, and players listen to match the numbers they hear with those on their game cards.

WORKBOOK

Pages 33–35

Language Note

Workbook p. 35: For additional oral practice with Exercise B, have students act out the conversations.

EXPANSION ACTIVITIES

1. Review Verbs in the Present Perfect Tense

   a. Write on the board:

> No. $\left\{ \begin{array}{l} \underline{\hspace{2cm}}\text{'s} \\ \underline{\hspace{2cm}}\text{'ve} \end{array} \right\}$ already \underline{\hspace{2cm}}.

b. Ask students each of the questions below. Have students respond, using the present perfect tense as shown in the model on the board. For example:

> You: Are you going to write your English composition tonight?
> Student: No. I've already written it.

Questions:

1. Are you going to write your English composition tonight?
2. Is (Mary) going to go to the dentist today?
3. Are your friends going to do their homework this afternoon?
4. Are you going to go jogging after school/work today?
5. It's late. Is your brother going to get dressed for the party?
6. Are you going to write to your uncle in (Chicago) this weekend?
7. Tomorrow is your sister's birthday. Are you going to give her a birthday gift?
8. Are you and your (husband) going to do your laundry this morning?
9. Sally's dog is sick. Is she going to take him to the vet today?
10. Are you going to see the new movie at the (Regency) theater?
11. (Tom) isn't feeling very well. Is he going to see the doctor this afternoon?
12. Are your friends (Barbara) and (Bill) going to get married this weekend?
13. Are you going to do your exercises tonight before you go to bed?
14. Is (Peter) going to eat lunch with us today?
15. Are you going to take your daughter to her piano lessons this afternoon?
16. Is Professor (Jones) going to give his famous lecture on American birds tonight?

2. *Don't You Remember?*

a. Write the following on the board:

A. You know, _____.
B. But $\left\{ \begin{array}{l} \underline{\quad}\text{'s} \\ \underline{\quad}\text{'ve} \end{array} \right\}$ already _____.
A. Really? When?
B. Don't you remember? _____ $\left\{ \begin{array}{l} \text{yesterday} \\ \text{last } \underline{\quad\quad} \\ \text{on } \underline{\quad\quad} \end{array} \right\}$.
A. Oh. That's right. I forgot.

b. Call on pairs of students to create conversations based on the model. Give one member of the pair the following opening lines as cues for the conversation:

1. You know, you should see the new movie at the Midtown Theater.
2. You know, Bobby should really write to his sister at camp.
3. You know, we should really do the laundry.
4. You know, you should take Professor Baker's European History course.
5. You know, we should give our secretary a raise.
6. You know, we should really eat that leftover chicken in the refrigerator.
7. You know, you should really wear that sweater your grandmother gave you.
8. You know, we should really go to the bank to get some cash.

Example:

A. You know, you should see the new movie at the Midtown Theater.
B. But I've already seen it.
A. Really? When?
B. Don't you remember? I saw it last weekend.
A. Oh. That's right. I forgot.

Text Page 38

READING: *We Can't Decide*

FOCUS

Present perfect tense

NEW VOCABULARY

go bowling   play cards
go dancing

PREVIEWING THE STORY (optional)

Have students talk about the story title and/or illustration. Introduce new vocabulary.

READING THE STORY

1. Have students read silently, or follow along silently as the story is read aloud by you, by one or more students, or on the tape.
2. Ask students if they have any questions; check understanding of vocabulary.
3. Check students' comprehension, using some or all of the following questions:

   a. What don't I want to do tonight?
   b. Why not?
   c. What doesn't Jack want to do tonight?
   d. Why not?
   e. What doesn't Nancy want to do tonight?

   f. Why not?
   g. What don't Betsy and Philip want to do tonight?
   h. Why not?
   i. Who wants to go dancing?
   j. Why not?

CHECK-UP

Group Conversation

1. Make sure students understand the instructions.
2. Have students work in groups to create new dialogs based on the model.
3. Call on the groups to present their dialogs to the class.

What's the Word?

1. been
2. seen
3. stayed
4. taken
5. drunk
6. eaten
7. rested
8. done

Text Page 39: *They Just Haven't Had the Time*

FOCUS

Practice with the present perfect tense:
- Negative statements
- Expressions with *in a long time*

INTRODUCING THE MODEL

1. Have students look at the model illustration.
2. Set the scene: "Two friends are talking."
3. Present the model.
4. Full-Class Choral Repetition.
5. Ask students if they have any questions; check understanding of new vocabulary: *in a long time, have the time.*
6. Group Choral Repetition.
7. Choral Conversation.
8. Call on one or two pairs of students to present the dialog. Check pronunciation of the contraction *haven't.*

   (For additional practice, do Choral Conversation in small groups or by rows.)

SIDE BY SIDE EXERCISES

These exercises require students to practice some of the past participles introduced in the previous lesson, as well as some new regular past participles. (See the footnote at the bottom of text page 39.)

Examples

1. A. Does Kathy like to go camping?
   B. Yes, she does. But she hasn't gone camping in a long time.
   A. Why not?
   B. She just hasn't had the time.

2. A. Does Robert like to do his English homework?
   B. Yes, he does. But he hasn't done his English homework in a long time.
   A. Why not?
   B. He just hasn't had the time.

1. **Exercise 1:** Review the past participle of the verb *go: go–went–**gone**.* Introduce the contraction *hasn't.* Call on two students to present the dialog. Then do Choral Repetition and Choral Conversation Practice.
2. **Exercise 2:** Review the past participle of the verb *do: do–did–**done**.* Same as above. Check pronunciation of the contraction *hasn't.*

3. **Exercises 3–8:**

> **New vocabulary and review of past participles:**   3.   *read, New York Times*
>   4.   *played, Monopoly*   5.   *taken*   6.   *made*   7.   *written*   8.   *seen*

Language Note

Exercise 3:   The forms of the verb *read* can be confusing to students since the pronunciation differs while the spelling is the same.

> read – read – read
> [rid]   [red]   [red]

Culture Note

Exercise 3:   The *New York Times* is one of the most widely read and respected newspapers in the United States.

Exercise 4:   Monopoly is a popular board game.

Either Full-Class Practice or Pair Practice

4. **Exercise 9:** Have students use the model as a guide to create their own conversations, using vocabulary of their choice. Encourage students to use dictionaries to find new words they want to use. This exercise can be done orally in class or for written homework. If you assign it for homework, you should do one example in class to make sure students understand what's expected. Have students present their conversations in class the next day.

WORKBOOK

Pages 36–37

EXPANSION ACTIVITIES

1. *Practice Changing Verbs to the Present Perfect Tense: Not This Week*

   a. Write on the board:

   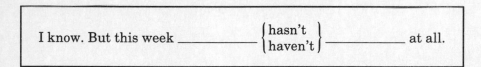

   b. Read each of the sentences below and have students complete the follow-up sentence on the board, using a negative present perfect tense verb. For example:

   > You: Mr. Jones usually says "hello" to us every week.
   > Students: I know. But this week he hasn't said "hello" at all.

   1. (Bill) usually arrives on time for class.
   2. I usually go to (Joe's Cafe) for lunch.
   3. (Sally) usually borrows my pen during class.
   4. (Walter) usually spends too much money.
   5. (Mrs. Blake) usually teaches very well.
   6. (Richard) usually studies English every day.
   7. I like to walk to school.
   8. (Jim) likes to wear his red tie.

9. The workers at the PRESTO Company usually work very hard.
10. (Ralph) usually talks to (Doris) after class.
11. (Carol) often helps her younger brother with his homework.
12. I usually do my laundry twice a week.
13. (Betsy) likes to cook chicken for dinner once a week.
14. The students in this class usually ask a lot of questions during class.
15. Every week (Norman) calls his parents in New York.
16. Sometimes you make mistakes in class.
17. (Kathy's) baby usually sleeps very well at night.
18. It usually rains a lot at this time of the year.
19. (Peggy) and her sister go jogging all the time.
20. (Frank's) children often watch too much TV.

An alternate way of doing this exercise is to write these statements on word cards and give them to students; then call on pairs of students.

2. *Talk about Plans for the Weekend*

a. Write on the board:

> A. What are you going to do this weekend?
> B. I'm not sure. I think I'll _____.
>   I haven't _____ in a long time.

b. Have pairs of students create conversations about what they're going to do this weekend. Students can practice independently in pairs and/or in front of the class. For example:

    A. What are you going to do this weekend?
    B. I'm not sure. I think I'll drive to the beach.
       I haven't driven to the beach in a long time.

Text Page 40: *Have You Seen the New Walt Disney Movie Yet?*

FOCUS

Practice with the present perfect tense:
- *Yes/no* questions and affirmative short answers
- Questions with *yet*

INTRODUCING THE MODEL

1. Have students look at the model illustration.
2. Set the scene: "Two students are talking about a new movie."
3. Present the model.
4. Full-Class Choral Repetition.
5. Ask students if they have any questions; check understanding of new vocabulary: *Walt Disney movie, yet.*

   ### Culture Note

   Walt Disney created cartoons and movies that are known and loved by children and adults around the world. He is also responsible for the development of *Disneyland* (in California) and *Disney World* (in Florida), which are major family entertainment centers and tourist attractions.

6. Group Choral Repetition.
7. Choral Conversation.
8. Call on one or two pairs of students to present the dialog.

   (For additional practice, do Choral Conversation in small groups or by rows.)

SIDE BY SIDE EXERCISES

In these exercises and the lessons that follow, new past participles that are not the same as the past tense form are given at the bottom of the page. Students can also refer to the list in the Appendix at the end of the student text.

Examples

1. A. Have you written your composition yet?
   B. Yes, I have. I wrote it yesterday.

2. A. Has Nancy ridden her new bicycle yet?
   B. Yes, she has. She rode it yesterday.

1. **Exercise 1:** Call on two students to present the dialog. Then do Choral Repetition and Choral Conversation Practice.
2. **Exercise 2:** Introduce the past participle of the verb *ride: ride–rode–**ridden***. Same as above.

3. **Exercises 3–9:**

> **New vocabulary:**   3. *driver's test*   6. *paycheck*   7. *make plans for*

Culture Note

> Exercise 3:   In order to receive a driver's license, all residents in the United States must pass a driver's test consisting of both a written test and a road test. The age when one may apply for a driver's license varies from state to state, but it generally ranges from 16 to 18 years of age.

Either Full-Class Practice or Pair Practice.

WORKBOOK

Page 38

EXPANSION ACTIVITIES

1. Practice Present Perfect Questions: New in Town

   a. Put on the board:

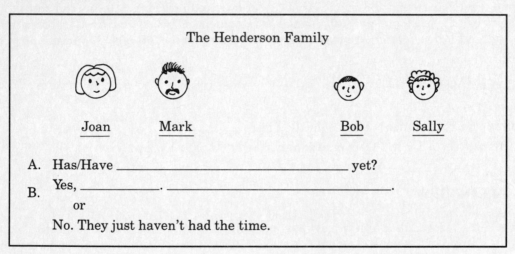

   The Henderson Family

   Joan   Mark   Bob   Sally

   A. Has/Have _____ yet?
   B. Yes, _____. _____.
       or
       No. They just haven't had the time.

   b. Set the scene: "Mr. and Mrs. Henderson and their children are new in town. They've just moved here, and they've been very busy. I think they're going to like (*name of your city*) very much."

   c. Have students create conversations in which they ask about all the experiences the Hendersons have had in their new city. For example, students can ask about getting an apartment, finding work, starting school, and going to local tourist sights and landmarks.

   Examples:

   > A. Have the Hendersons found an apartment yet?
   > B. Yes, they have. They found an apartment (on Maple Street).

   > A. Have the children started school yet?
   > B. Yes, they have. They started school last month, and they like it very much.

   > A. Have they visited the museum yet?
   > B. No. They just haven't had the time.

2. More Present Perfect Practice: Going Abroad

a. Write the following on the board:

```
Have you _____?

get your passport
apply for your visa
buy _____ for the trip
make hotel reservations
pack
buy your plane ticket
_____
```

b. Divide the class into pairs and set the scene: "One of you is going on a trip and you have a lot of things to do before you go. Your friend is trying to help you remember everything you have to do."

c. Using cues on the board, have pairs create conversations about the trip one of them is going to take.

d. After the students have *rehearsed* their conversations, call on several pairs to present their conversations to the class. For example:

    A. Where are you going?
    B. To China.
    A. When are you leaving?
    B. Next month.
    A. Have you gotten your passport yet?
    B. Yes, I have. I got it yesterday.
    A. Have you bought clothes for the trip?
    B. Yes. I've bought everything I need.
    A. Have you packed yet?
    B. No, I haven't. I'll pack the night before I leave.
    A. Have you learned any Chinese phrases?
    B. Yes. I've learned how to say "Hello" and "Good-bye."

Text Page 41: *Has Peter Left for Work Yet?*

FOCUS

Practice with the present perfect tense:
- Negative short answers
- Questions with *yet*

INTRODUCING THE MODEL

1. Have students look at the model illustration.
2. Set the scene: "Two people are talking about Peter."
3. Present the model.
4. Full-Class Choral Repetition.
5. Ask students if they have any questions; check understanding of new vocabulary: *leave for work*.
6. Group Choral Repetition.
7. Choral Conversation.
8. Call on one or two pairs of students to present the dialog.

   (For additional practice, do Choral Conversation in small groups or by rows.)

SIDE BY SIDE EXERCISES

Examples

1. A. Has Mildred taken her medicine yet?
   B. No, she hasn't. She has to take it/her medicine now.

2. A. Have you finished your homework?
   B. No, I haven't. I have to finish it/my homework now.

1. **Exercise 1:** Introduce the new word *medicine*. Call on two students to present the dialog. Then do Choral Repetition and Choral Conversation Practice.
2. **Exercise 2:** Same as above.
3. **Exercises 3–9:**

   New vocabulary: 8. *speak–spoke–**spoken*** 9. *pay–paid–paid*

   Either Full-Class Practice or Pair Practice.

WORKBOOK

Pages 39–41

EXPANSION ACTIVITIES

1. **Role Play:** *Have you* _____ *yet?*

   a. Write the following roles/situations on word cards:

      1. parent–child
      2. boss–employee
      3. teacher–student
      4. student–student (before taking an examination)
      5. two friends (one of them is going to take a vacation soon)
      6. two neighbors (talking about the landlord)
      7. nurse–patient (in a hospital)

   b. Divide the class into pairs and have each pair create a 4-line dialog that begins:

      "Have you _____ yet?"

      The dialogs should reflect the roles and contexts which the students have been given on the word cards.

   c. Have each pair present their dialog to the class. Then have the other students guess what roles they're playing: Are they friends? Is a teacher talking to a student? For example:

(parent–child)	A.	Have you cleaned your room yet?
	B.	No, I haven't. But I'm going to clean it tonight.
	A.	Well, please don't forget. I've already asked you two times.
	B.	Don't worry. I won't forget.

(boss–employee)	A.	Have you typed those letters yet?
	B.	Yes, I have. I just finished a few minutes ago.
	A.	Can I see them, please?
	B.	Certainly. Here they are.

2. *Vocabulary Review and Present Perfect Practice*

   a. Write the following on the board:

	Have/Has _____?	
take his medicine	finish her homework	get up
say good-bye	feed the dog	call her boss
go to bed	speak to your landlord	pay his electric bill

   b. Read the situations below and call on students to respond, using the present perfect and an appropriate phrase from the list on the board. For example:

You:	I don't have any heat in my apartment!
Student:	Have you spoken to your landlord?

   Situations:

      1. I don't have any heat in my apartment!
         (Have you spoken to your landlord?)
      2. The lights in Henry's house won't go on.
         (Has he paid his electric bill?)
      3. Walter is feeling very sick.
         (Has he taken his medicine?)
      4. Mary's alarm clock is ringing.
         (Has she gotten up?)

5. Fido is very hungry and is barking very loudly.
   (Have you fed the dog?)
6. My daughter wants to watch TV.
   (Has she finished her homework?)
7. Alice has decided to stay home from work today.
   (Has she called her boss?)
8. Bobby is very tired.
   (Has he gone to bed?)
9. Margaret and Michael are leaving for the airport.
   (Have they said good-bye?)

Text Page 42

READING: *Working Overtime*

FOCUS

Present perfect tense

NEW VOCABULARY

as for me	mailroom
bookkeeper	office clerk
co-worker	surprised
desk	typical

PREVIEWING THE STORY (optional)

Have students talk about the story title and/or illustration. Introduce new vocabulary.

READING THE STORY

1. Have students read silently, or follow along silently as the story is read aloud by you, by one or more students, or on the tape.
2. Ask students if they have any questions; check understanding of vocabulary.

   Culture Note

   Overtime is any work done over the 40-hour work week. Workers are usually paid more per hour than their normal salary, usually one and a half times their hourly wage.

3. Check students' comprehension, using some or all of the following questions:

   a. Have the employees of the Goodwell Computer Company gone home yet?
   b. Why not?
   c. Why hasn't the secretary gone home yet?
   d. Why hasn't the bookkeeper gone home yet?
   e. Why haven't the office clerks gone home yet?
   f. Why hasn't the boss gone home yet?
   g. Why hasn't the custodian gone home yet?
   h. Why hasn't he cleaned all the offices?
   i. Why isn't he surprised?

CHECK-UP

Q & A

1. Call on a pair of students to present the model.
2. Have students work in pairs to create new dialogs.
3. Call on pairs to present their new dialogs to the class.

What's the Word?

1. seen
   saw

2. eaten
   ate

3. gone
   has/went

4. spoken
   have/spoke

5. made
   made

6. read
   read

7. taken
   hasn't/took/he hasn't taken

8. finished
   has/gone

Text Pages 43–44: *Have You Seen Any Good Movies Recently?*

FOCUS

- Review of the present perfect tense
- Expressions with *recently* and *ever*

INTRODUCING THE MODEL

1. Have students look at the model illustration.
2. Set the scene: "It's Friday, and two students are talking about their plans for tonight."
3. Present the model.
4. Full-Class Choral Repetition.
5. Ask students if they have any questions; check understanding of new vocabulary: *recently, ever.*

   Culture Note

   Superman is a well-known cartoon hero.

6. Group Choral Repetition.
7. Choral Conversation.
8. Call on one or two pairs of students to present the dialog.

   (For additional practice, do Choral Conversation in small groups or by rows.)

SIDE BY SIDE EXERCISES

In these exercises students use any names of movies, plays, or books they wish.

Example

> 1. A. What are you going to do tonight?
>   B. I'm not sure. I really want to read a good book.
>   I haven't read a good book in a long time.
>   A. What book are you going to read?
>   B. I don't know. Have you read any good books recently?
>   A. Yes, I have. I read a VERY good book just last week.
>   B. Really? What book did you read?
>   A. I read (*War and Peace*).
>   B. And you liked it?
>   A. I LOVED it! I think it's one of the BEST books I've ever read.

1. **Exercise 1:** Call on two students to present the dialog. Then do Choral Repetition and Choral Conversation Practice.
2. **Exercises 2–4:** Either Full-Class Practice or Pair Practice.

WORKBOOK

Pages 42–44

> Workbook p. 42:   For additional oral practice with Exercise G, have students act out the conversations.

EXPANSION ACTIVITIES

1. **Role Play: *Meeting a Famous Person***

    a. Ask students to name a few of their favorite writers, actors/actresses, dancers, singers, or other artists.

    b. Write on the board:

    A. Excuse me. Aren't you _____?
    B. Yes, I am.
    A. (Mr./Mrs./Miss/Ms.) _____. I've always wanted to meet you!
        I've _____ all your _____s, and I think they're
        the _____ _____s I've ever _____.
    B. Thank you very much.

    (Have students expand the dialog.)

    ---

    c. Set the scene: "Imagine that you're walking down the street and you see a famous person you have always wanted to meet."

    d. Call on pairs of students to role play this *chance encounter*. Student A can pretend to meet the writer/actor/etc. he or she really admires. For example:

    A. Excuse me. Aren't you Sophia Loren?
    B. Yes, I am.
    A. Ms. Loren, I've always wanted to meet you! I've seen all your movies,
        and I think they're the best movies I've ever seen.
    B. Thank you very much.

    (Possible expansion)

    A. Ms. Loren. Could you possibly do me a favor?
    B. Of course. What is it?
    A. Could you please give me your autograph?
    B. I'll be happy to.

2. **Asking for and Giving Recommendations**

    a. Write the following conversational model on the board:

    A. Can you recommend a good $\begin{cases} \text{book} \\ \text{movie} \\ \text{restaurant} \\ \text{hotel} \\ \text{TV program} \end{cases}$?

    B. Yes. _____ is a good _____. As a matter of fact,
        I think it's one of the best _____s I've ever _____.
    A. _____.
    B. _____.
    A. That's great! Thanks for the recommendation.

    ---

b. Call on pairs of students to create conversations based on the model, using names of real books, movies, restaurants, hotels, etc. For example:

    A. Can you recommend a good restaurant?
    B. Yes. Luigi's is a good restaurant. As a matter of fact, I think it's one of the best restaurants I've ever eaten at.
    A. Is it very expensive?
    B. No, not at all.
    A. That's great! Thanks for the recommendation.

    A. Can you recommend a good hotel?
    B. Yes. The Windsor is a good hotel. As a matter of fact, I think it's one of the best hotels I've ever stayed at.
    A. Where is it located?
    B. It's on Jackson Boulevard, near the park.
    A. That's great! Thanks for the recommendation.

3. *Write a Review*

a. Have students pretend they work for a newspaper and write a review of one of the following:

    a movie they've seen
    a play they've seen
    a book they've read
    a restaurant where they've eaten

b. Have students read their reviews to the class and have others react to the reviews by agreeing or disagreeing, or perhaps by asking for more information about the movie, play, book, or restaurant.

READING: *Sharon Likes New York*

FOCUS

Present perfect tense

NEW VOCABULARY

do a lot of things	take a tour	United Nations
Empire State Building	top	World Trade Center

PREVIEWING THE STORY (optional)

Have students talk about the story title and/or illustration. Introduce new vocabulary.

READING THE STORY

1. Have students read silently, or follow along silently as the story is read aloud by you, by one or more students, or on the tape.
2. Ask students if they have any questions; check understanding of vocabulary.
3. Check students' comprehension, using one or both of the following questions:

   a. What has Sharon done in New York?
   b. What hasn't she done yet?

CHECK-UP

Listening

Have students complete the exercises as you play the tape or read the following:

1. Sharon is on vacation in San Francisco. She's checking her list of things to do while she's on vacation. On the list below, check the things Sharon has already done.

   Sharon has already seen the Golden Gate Bridge. She hasn't visited Golden Gate Park yet. She took a tour of Alcatraz Prison yesterday. She's going to go to Chinatown tomorrow. She's eaten at Fisherman's Wharf, and she hasn't had time to buy souvenirs yet.

   ✓ see the Golden Gate Bridge   ✓ take a tour of Alcatraz Prison
   ✓ eat at Fisherman's Wharf

2. Alan is a secretary in a very busy office. He's checking his list of things to do before 5 P.M. on Friday. On the list below, check the things Alan has already done.

Alan has called Mrs. Porter. He has to type the letter to the Ajax Insurance Company. He's gone to the bank. He hasn't taken the mail to the post office. He cleaned the coffee machine, and he's going to speak to the boss about his salary.

✓ call Mrs. Porter   ✓ go to the bank   ✓ clean the coffee machine

3. It's Saturday, and Judy and Paul Johnson are doing lots of things around the house. They're checking the list of things they have to do today. On the list below, check the things they've already done.

Judy and Paul haven't done the laundry. They have to wash the kitchen windows. They've paid the bills. They'll clean the garage later. They couldn't fix the bathroom sink, but they vacuumed the living room.

✓ pay the bills   ✓ vacuum the living room

IN YOUR OWN WORDS

1. Make sure students understand the instructions.
2. Have students do the activity as written homework, using a dictionary for any new words they wish to use.
3. Have students present and discuss what they have written, in pairs or as a class.

Page 33   A.   NOT TODAY

1. He's, gone
   He went
2. I've, written
   I wrote
3. She's, eaten
   She ate
4. We've, done
   We did
5. He's, worn
   He wore
6. They've, taken
   They took
7. He's, given
   He gave
8. We've, spent
   We spent
9. I've, bought
   I bought
10. She's, swum
    She swam
11. He's, cooked
    He cooked
12. They've, gone
    They went

Page 35   B.   WHAT ARE THEY SAYING?

1. I've, taken
   I took
2. I've, seen
   I saw
3. I've, gone
   You went
4. He's, gotten
   He got

Page 36   C.   IN A LONG TIME

1. hasn't eaten
2. haven't danced
3. hasn't gone
4. haven't practiced
5. hasn't cleaned
6. haven't seen
7. haven't done
8. hasn't fixed
9. haven't taken
10. hasn't read
11. haven't studied
12. haven't written
13. haven't had

Page 38   D.   WHAT ARE THEY SAYING?

1. Have, gone, I have
2. Has, written, she has
3. Have, seen, we have
4. Has, worn, he has
5. Have, taken, they have
6. Have, made, we have
7. Has, met, she has
8. Have, done, I have

9. Have, gotten, they have
10. Have, given, I have
11. Has, ridden, he has

Page 39   E.   A LOT OF THINGS TO DO

1. He's already gone shopping.
2. He hasn't cleaned his apartment yet.
3. He hasn't gotten a haircut yet.
4. He's already baked bread.
5. He hasn't made dessert yet.
6. He's already fixed the stereo.

7. They haven't done their laundry yet.
8. They've already paid their electric bill.
9. They haven't packed their suitcases yet.
10. They've already returned their library books.
11. They've already bought a new tennis racket.
12. They haven't said good-bye to their neighbors yet.

13. She's already written to Mrs. Peters.
14. She hasn't called Miss Watson yet.
15. She's already taken Mr. Warren to lunch.
16. She hasn't met with Mr. Grant yet.
17. She's already sent income tax forms to the new employees.
18. She hasn't fired Mr. Smith yet.

Page 41   F.   *IS* OR *HAS*?

1.	has	11.	is
2.	is	12.	has
3.	is	13.	is
4.	has	14.	has
5.	is	15.	has
6.	is	16.	is
7.	has	17.	has
8.	is	18.	is
9.	is	19.	is
10.	has	20.	has

1. wrote, hasn't written
   she'll
2. Have
   I haven't, did
   got, he's
   rode
3. seen
   haven't, saw
   you see
   seen
4. Have
   I have, spoke
   did
   hasn't
   going to

5. did
   gave
   are you going to buy
   spent
   did you
   bought
6. I'm not, taken
   got, Have
   I have, ate, washed/done

Page 44 I. __ULIA'S BROKEN T__PEWRITER

1.

> Judy,
>   Did I leave my blue and Yellow Jacket at Your house Yesterday after the Jazz concert? I Just can't find it anywhere.
>   Julia

2.

> Dear Jennifer,
>   We're sorry You and Joe can't visit us this June. Do You think You can come in July? We really enJoyed Your visit last Year.
>   Julia

3.

> Jeff,
>   Jack and I are out Jogging, but we'll be back in Just a few minutes. Make Yourself comfortable. You can wait for us in the Yard. If You're thirsty, take some Juice from the refrigerator.
>   Julia

4.

> Dear Jane,
>   Thank You very much for the beautiful paJamas you sent Jimmy. He received them Yesterday. Jimmy is too Young to write to You himself, but he says, "Thank You." I'm sure he'll enJoy wearing his new paJamas on cold January nights.
>   Love,
>   Julia

5.

> Jack,
>   We need a Jar of Jelly, a large can of orange Juice, and some Yogurt. Would You please buy them when You go to the store today?
>   Julia

6.

> Dear Janet,
>   We got a letter from George Jackson Just last week. He's really enJoying college this Year. His favorite subJects are German and Japanese. He's looking for a Job in New York as a Journalist, but he hasn't found one Yet.
>   Julia

GRAMMAR

Since/For

We've known each other	since	three o'clock. yesterday afternoon. last week. 1960. we were in high school.
	for	three hours. two days. a week. a long time.

Irregular Verbs

be– was –been know–knew–known

Present Perfect vs. Present Tense

I know Mrs. Potter.
I've **known** her since I was a little boy.

Present Perfect vs. Past Tense

Ralph was a painter.
He's **been** a carpenter for the last ten years.

FUNCTIONS

Asking for and Reporting Information

How long *has your neck been stiff*?
  For *more than a week*.

Do you know *Mrs. Potter*?
  Yes, I do. I've known *her* for a long time.

How long have you *known each other*?
  We've known each other for *two years*.
  We've known each other since *1960*.

Has *Ralph* always been *a carpenter*?
  No. *He's* been *a carpenter for the last ten years*.
  Before that, *he* was *a painter*.

Have *you* always *taught history*?
  No. *I've taught history* since *1980*.
  Before that, *I taught geography*.

Do you still *live on Main Street*?
  No. I haven't *lived on Main Street for several years*.
Where do you *live* NOW?
  I *live on River Road*.

Are you still *a barber*?
  No. I haven't been *a barber for several years*.
What do you do NOW?
  I'm a *taxi driver*.

So how are you feeling today, *George*?
  Not very well, *Dr. Fernando*.
What seems to be the problem?
  My neck is stiff.

What is your present address?
How long have you lived there?
What was your last address?
How long did you live there?

Tell me, _____.
Tell me, *Tony*, _____.
And how about YOU?

Responding to Information

Really?

Oh, really? That's interesting.

Indicating Understanding

I see.

Greeting People

George!
  Tony!

How have you been?
  Fine. And how about YOU?
Everything's fine with me, too.

Expressing Surprise-Disbelief

I can't believe it's you!

Expressing Agreement

That's right, *George*.

Leave Taking

Well, *George*, I'm afraid I have to go now. We should
  get together soon.
  Good idea, *Tony*.

NEW VOCABULARY

accent
army
art
assistant manager
astronaut
astronomy
bachelor
barber
been
black and blue
body
bottom
carpenter
cashier
clerk
computer technology
corporation
count
dedicated (adj)
Democrats
department
dizzy
engaged
engineer
everything
feel dizzy
fever

for the past *24 hours*
fortunate
geography
go fishing
guitarist
have the measles
high fever
interested (in)
knee
lottery
manager
measles
medical school
modern art
more than *a week*
musician
Nashville
neck
own (v)
pain
past
patient (n)
personal computer
Picasso
present (adj)
Republicans

salesperson
satellite
saxophone
Singapore
space
stiff
store manager
successful
swollen
take time
taxi driver
technology
Tennessee
termites
vice-president
waiting room
Watergate

Good idea.
happily married
in love
It's been a long time.
So . . .
start at the bottom
"the birds and the bees"
work *his* way up to the top

Text Pages 48–49: *How Long?*

FOCUS

Present perfect tense:
- Questions with *how long*
- Expressions with *for* and *since*

INTRODUCING THE MODEL

There are two model conversations. Introduce and practice each separately. For each model:

1. Have students look at the model illustration.
2. Set the scene:

    1st model: "Two people who are 'in love' are talking to a friend."
    2nd model: "The woman in bed isn't feeling well, and her friend has come to visit her."

3. Present the model.
4. Full-Class Choral Repetition.
5. Ask students if they have any questions; check understanding of new vocabulary:

    1st model: *how long, known, each other*
    2nd model: *been*

Language Note

Time expressions with *for* and *since* are commonly used with the present perfect tense. *For* is used with expressions describing a period of time. For example:

> *We've known each other for two years.*
> *He's been married for a long time.*

Since is used with expressions describing a definite point in time. For example:

> *I've been sick since last Thursday.*
> *They've been married since 1945.*
> *He's played the piano since he was eight years old.*
> *I've had a fever since I got up yesterday morning.*
> *Janet has known all the people in her apartment building since the fire last year.*

6. Group Choral Repetition.
7. Choral Conversation.
8. Call on one or two pairs of students to present the dialog.

    (For additional practice, do Choral Conversation in small groups or by rows.)

9. Further substitution practice:

    a. After the 1st model, call on pairs of students to present the model again, using some of the other expressions under *for* in the box at the top of the page. For example:

        a long time

        A. How long have you known each other?
        B. We've known each other for a long time.

b. After the 2nd model, same as above, using some of the expressions under *since* in the box at the top of the page. For example:

> *last week*
>
> A. How long have you been sick?
> B. I've been sick since last week.

SIDE BY SIDE EXERCISES

Examples

> 1. A. How long have Don and Patty known each other?
>   B. They've known each other for three years.
>
> 2. A. How long have Mr. and Mrs. Peterson been married?
>   B. They've been married since 1945.

1. **Exercise 1:** Call on two students to present the dialog. Then do Choral Repetition and Choral Conversation Practice.

2. **Exercise 2:** Same as above.

3. **Exercises 3–12:**

> **New vocabulary:** 5. *have the measles* 7. *satellite, space* 8. *own* (v)
> 10. *interested in, astronomy* 11. *computer technology*

Either Full-Class Practice or Pair Practice.

WORKBOOK

Pages 45–46

EXPANSION ACTIVITIES

1. *Quick Review of* **For** *vs.* **Since**

   a. Write on the board:

   > for _____
   > since _____

   Check students' understanding of how these words are used.

   b. Read each time expression below. Have students listen and form an expression with the correct word. For example:

You: a long time	You: last week
Students: for a long time	Students: since last week

1.	yesterday	(since)	8.	a long time	(for)
2.	two hours	(for)	9.	three and a half months	(for)
3.	a few minutes	(for)	10.	a quarter past three	(since)
4.	this morning	(since)	11.	ten years	(for)
5.	1981	(since)	12.	Wednesday	(since)
6.	several weeks	(for)	13.	last month	(since)
7.	ten o'clock last night	(since)	14.	three days	(for)
			15.	1988	(since)

2. **More Practice with For and Since**

a. Write the following on the board or on a handout for the class:

Model 1:   These two people have known each other since _____.

Exercise 1:   Don and Patty have known each other since _____.

Exercise 2:   Mr. and Mrs. Peterson have been married for _____.

Exercise 6:   Mrs. Brown has been a teacher since _____.

Exercise 7:   There have been satellites in space for _____.

Exercise 8:   She's owned her own car since _____.

Exercise 9:   John has owned his own house for _____.

Exercise 12: He's been in jail for _____.

---

b. Remind students: "This year is (1990)."

c. Tell students that, based on what year this is, they should go back to text pages 48 and 49 and answer the questions about the characters. Do the first one with them. For example:

"This year is (1990). They've known each other for two years.
Therefore: These two people have known each other since (1988)."

d. Call on individual students to give their answers.

Variations: You can also do this as a competition.

1. Divide the class into teams.

2. Each team works together to figure out the answers to the questions.

3. Call on each team to give their answers. A team gets 10 points for each correct answer. The team with the most points wins the game.

3. **Students Talk about Themselves**

a. Write on the board:

---

study _____

live in _____

be interested in _____

own _____

have _____

be _____

know _____

---

b. Have students ask and answer questions about each other with *how long*. Have students use the verbs on the board in the present perfect tense. Call on pairs of students or divide the class into pairs. For example:

A. How long have you lived in (Tokyo)?
B. I've lived in (Tokyo) for ten years.

A. How long have you owned (a car)?
B. I've owned (a car) since 1988.

READING: *A Very Dedicated Doctor*

FOCUS

> • Present perfect tense
> • Since/For

NEW VOCABULARY

black and blue	more than *a week*
body	neck
dedicated (adj)	pain
dizzy	past
feel dizzy	patient (n)
fever	stiff
for the past *24 hours*	swollen
knee	take time
	waiting room

PREVIEWING THE STORY (optional)

Have students talk about the story title and/or illustrations. Introduce new vocabulary.

READING THE STORY

1. Have students read silently, or follow along silently as the story is read aloud by you, by one or more students, or on the tape.
2. Ask students if they have any questions; check understanding of vocabulary.
3. Check students' comprehension, using some or all of the following questions:

   a. What's the matter with George?
   b. What's the matter with Martha?
   c. What's the matter with Lenny?
   d. What's the matter with Carol?
   e. What's the matter with Bob?
   f. What's the matter with Bill?
   g. What's the matter with Tommy and Julie?
   h. How long has Dr. Fernando been in his office?
   i. What don't his patients know?
   j. What's the matter with him?
   k. Why hasn't he taken time to stay at home and rest?

CHECK-UP

Q & A

1. Call on a pair of students to present the model.
2. Have students work in pairs to create new dialogs.
3. Call on pairs to present their new dialogs to the class.

Choose

I.			
1.	a	5.	a
2.	b	6.	b
3.	b	7.	a
4.	a	8.	a

II.			
1.	b	4.	a
2.	a	5.	b
3.	b	6.	b

Text Pages 52–53: *Since I Was a Little Boy*

FOCUS

> Present perfect tense:
> * Contrast with the present tense
> * *Since* expressions

GETTING READY

Contrast the simple present tense and the present perfect tense.

1. Put these cues on the board:

Lucy

speak English
interested/astronomy
married
own/house
work/restaurant

2. Make two statements about each cue: one in the present tense and one in the present perfect tense. For example:

   "Lucy speaks English."
   "She's spoken English since she was young."

   "Lucy is interested in astronomy."
   "She's been interested in astronomy for a long time."

3. Point to each cue and call on one or more students to tell about Lucy in the same way.

INTRODUCING THE MODEL

There are two model conversations. Introduce and practice each separately. For each model:

1. Have students look at the model illustration.
2. Set the scene:

   1st model: "Two joggers are talking about Mrs. Potter."
   2nd model: "A man is talking to a couple at a party."

3. Present the model.
4. Full-Class Choral Repetition.
5. Ask students if they have any questions; check understanding of new vocabulary:

   2nd model: *engaged*

   Culture Note

   In traditional U.S. culture, a couple who are planning to get married may announce their intentions by becoming *engaged* to be married. The man may also give the woman an engagement ring.

6. Group Choral Repetition.

7. Choral Conversation.

8. Call on one or two pairs of students to present the dialog.

(For additional practice, do Choral Conversation in small groups or by rows.)

SIDE BY SIDE EXERCISES

Examples

1. A. Does your brother play the piano?
   B. Yes, he does. He's played the piano for a long time.
   A. Oh, really? That's interesting. Tell me, how long has he played the piano?
   B. He's played the piano since he was eight years old.

2. A. Is your friend Victor a professional musician?
   B. Yes, he is. He's been a professional musician for a long time.
   A. Oh, really? That's interesting. Tell me, how long has he been a professional musician?
   B. He's been a professional musician since he finished college.

1. **Exercise 1:** Call on two students to present the dialog. Then do Choral Repetition and Choral Conversation Practice.

2. **Exercise 2:** Introduce the new word *musician*. Same as above.

3. **Exercises 3–12:**

   New vocabulary: 3. *personal computer* 4. *modern art*
   7. *know how to* 8. *count* 9. *own* (v), *own business* 11. *termites*
   12. *"the birds and the bees"*

   Language Note

   Exercise 2: A professional musician is someone who plays an instrument for a living.

   Culture Notes

   Exercise 4: Pablo Picasso is a famous 20th-century artist.

   Exercise 12: The euphemistic expression "the birds and the bees" is used in polite conversation to refer to the *facts of life* or *where babies come from*.

   Either Full-Class Practice or Pair Practice.

WORKBOOK

Pages 47–49

EXPANSION ACTIVITIES

1. *Practice* Since *Expressions*

   a. Write the following cues on the board:

```
I know. _____ since _____.

finish high school/college
leave the army
start this class
be _____ years old
read a book about it
see a movie about it
hear a lecture about it
go _____ing and had an accident
go to work at _____
retire
move to _____
take _____ lessons
```

b. Read the present tense statements below. Have two or more students respond by saying "I know" followed by a statement in the present perfect tense with *since*. Students can use any of the cues on the board for ideas. For example:

> You: Carmen has long hair.
> Student: I know. She's had long hair since she was ten years old.

Statements:

1. Bill works at the bank.
2. The Smiths live in London.
3. Susan and her family have an apartment.
4. Roger has a broken leg.
5. Bill and Mary are married.
6. Linda's daughter speaks English.
7. My neighbors play tennis very well.
8. Henry Jones wants to be a nurse.
9. Mrs. Potter wants to be a professional musician.
10. Kathy is very interested in history.

2. *Guess Who: Students Talk about Themselves*

a. Write on the board:

```
  ⎧ like            ⎫
I ⎨ am interested in ⎬ _____.
  ⎩                 ⎭

  ⎧ know how to ⎫
I ⎨ can         ⎬ _____.
  ⎩            ⎭

I play _____.
I'm a _____.
I want to be a _____.
I have _____.
```

b. Have each student write three sentences about himself or herself, using some of the cues on the board. For example:

> *I'm interested in computers.*
> *I play the guitar.*
> *I have a pet bird.*

c. Have students fold their papers and give them to you. Mix them up and give each student someone else's paper.

d. Call on students to read the sentences. Then have the class guess who wrote them.

e. After the class has identified the person who wrote the statements, have students ask that person any questions they wish, using *how long*.

3. Role Play: At a Party

a. Write the following on the board:

> interested in?
> live?
> work?
> how long?

b. Divide the class into pairs.

c. Tell each pair that they've just met at a party. Have them create a role play, using the key expressions on the board.

d. Call on pairs to present their conversations to the class.

Text Pages 54–55: *Has Ralph Always Been a Carpenter?*

FOCUS

Present perfect tense:
- Contrast with the past tense
- Review of *yes/no* questions

INTRODUCING THE MODEL

There are two model conversations. Introduce and practice each separately. For each model:

1. Have students look at the model illustration.
2. Set the scene:

   1st model: "Two people are talking about Ralph."
   2nd model: "A student is talking to her teacher."

3. Present the model.
4. Full-Class Choral Repetition.
5. Ask students if they have any questions; check understanding of new vocabulary:

   1st model: *carpenter*
   2nd model: *geography*
6. Group Choral Repetition.
7. Choral Conversation.
8. Call on one or two pairs of students to present the dialog.

   (For additional practice, do Choral Conversation in small groups or by rows.)

SIDE BY SIDE EXERCISES

Examples

1. A. Has Fred always been thin?
   B. No, he's been thin for the last three years. Before that, he was heavy.

2. A. Has Roberta always had short hair?
   B. No, she's had short hair since she finished college. Before that, she had long hair.

1. **Exercise 1:** Call on two students to present the dialog. Then do Choral Repetition and Choral Conversation Practice.
2. **Exercise 2:** Introduce the new word *college.* Same as above.
3. **Exercises 3–10:**

   New vocabulary: 3. *the past few years*   4. *Democrats, Watergate, Republicans*
   5. *a Boston accent, a New York accent*   7. *astronaut*   8. *store manager, cashier*
   9. *fire*   10. *lottery*

Exercise 3: *The past few years* and other periods of time can be expressed this way:

$$\text{the past few} \begin{cases} minutes \\ hours \\ weeks \\ months \end{cases}$$

Culture Note

Exercise 5: North-American accents can vary widely along geographic and social lines.

Either Full-Class Practice or Pair Practice.

4. **Answer These Questions:** Call on several pairs of students to ask and answer questions 1–6 at the bottom of text page 41.

WORKBOOK

Pages 50–51

EXPANSION ACTIVITIES

1. *Contrasting Past and Present Perfect Tenses*

   a. Write on the board:

   > _____ from _____ to _____.
   >
   > Since then, $\begin{cases} \text{he's} \\ \text{she's} \\ \text{they've} \end{cases}$ _____.

   b. Write on the board or on large word cards:

1. Martha secretary 1981–1986 work with computers '86–now	4. Mr. Smith work 1945–1985 retire '85–now
2. Janet study art 1977–1983 painter '83–now	5. Ted college 1983–1987 work '87–now
3. George and his family Boston 1980–1984 Miami '84–now	6. Jane and Richard marry 1959–1979 divorce '79–now

   c. Point to the first set of cues and tell about Martha:

   "Martha was a secretary from 1981 to 1986. Since then, she's worked with computers."

   Then ask questions with *how long* in both the past and present perfect tenses. For example:

   "How long was Martha a secretary?"
   "How long has she worked with computers?"

d. Point to each of the other cues and call on students to:

> Tell about the person using the model on the board.
> Ask questions with *how long*.

e. Change the model on the board so that it reads:

> _____ from _____ to _____.
> Since then, I've _____.

Have students talk about themselves, using this model. For example:

> "I lived on Central Street from 1985 to 1987.
> Since then, I've lived on Green Street."

2. **Summarizing with the Present Perfect Tense**

Have students listen as you read each situation below. Then call on a student to *summarize* what happened, using the present perfect tense. There may be more than one correct way to summarize what happened. For example:

Situation:

> "Bill saw Jim this morning. He saw him again at lunch. Then he saw him again in the parking lot."

Summary:

> "Bill has seen Jim three times today."
>   or
> "Bill has seen Jim several times/a lot today."

Situations:

a. I called Gloria this morning, and I called her again this afternoon.
b. Sally wrote two letters to the PRESTO Company last week, and she wrote them another one this week.
c. We saw Mr. and Mrs. Grant at a basketball game on Tuesday night and at a concert on Thursday night.
d. Richard studied French in high school. He studied German in college. And last year he studied Japanese.
e. Mrs. Phillips went to Europe in 1985. She visited Europe again in 1988.
f. Mr. Perkins gave a piano lesson at 8 o'clock this morning, at noon, and again at 2 o'clock this afternoon.
g. Larry is reading a lot this year in school. He read four books last semester. And he read two more books last month.
h. Joe came to class late yesterday. He came to class late again today.
i. Janet's aunt sent her a birthday gift this week. Her friend sent her one, too.
j. Mrs. Peters had a baby girl in 1979. In 1984 she had a boy.
k. My students did very well on their English tests last semester. They did well on their tests this semester, too.

3. **Students Talk about Themselves**

a. Write on the board:

> I've _____ (since/for) _____.
> Before that, _____.
> _____.

b. Tell something about yourself, using the model on the board. For example:

"I've taught in this school for twelve years.
Before that, I taught at the (Park School).
I like this school much better."

"I've lived in (Los Angeles) since 1985.
Before that, I lived in (Chicago).
I moved to Los Angeles because of the warm weather.
I'm glad I moved here."

c. Call on students to tell something about themselves.

Variations: Have students do this activity in pairs. Then call on students to tell about their partners.

READING: *A Wonderful Family*

FOCUS

Present perfect vs. Present tense

NEW VOCABULARY

bachelor	happily married
engineer	medical school
fortunate	Singapore
guitarist	successful

PREVIEWING THE STORY (optional)

Have students talk about the story title and/or illustration. Introduce new vocabulary.

READING THE STORY

1. Have students read silently, or follow along silently as the story is read aloud by you, by one or more students, or on the tape.
2. Ask students if they have any questions; check understanding of vocabulary.
3. Check students' comprehension, using some or all of the following questions:

   a. What does Ruth do?
   b. How long has she been an engineer?
   c. How long have Ruth and Pablo been married?
   d. What does Pablo do?
   e. How long has he known how to play the guitar?
   f. What does David do?
   g. How long has he been interested in computers?
   h. What does Rita do?
   i. How long has she been a doctor?
   j. Is Herbert married?
   k. What does Herbert do?
   l. Have Mr. and Mrs. Patterson seen him recently?

CHECK-UP

True or False?

1. True
2. False
3. True
4. False
5. True
6. False

Listening

Have students complete the exercises as you play the tape or read the following:

Listen to the conversation and choose the answer that is true.

1. A. How long have you had a toothache?
   B. For three days. (b)

2. A. How long was your knee swollen?
   B. For a week. (a)

3. A. Has your father always been an engineer?
   B. No, he hasn't. (a)

4. A. How long have you known how to skate?
   B. Since I was a teenager. (b)

5. A. Did you live in Rome for a long time?
   B. Yes. Five years. (b)

6. A. How long has Jim been interested in Greek literature?
   B. Since he lived in Greece. (a)

7. A. Is Betty still in the hospital?
   B. Oh, I forgot to tell you. She's been home for two days. (a)

8. A. Have you liked country music for a long time?
   B. Yes. I've liked country music since I moved to Nashville seven years ago. (a)

Text Page 57

READING: *Working Their Way Up to the Top*

FOCUS

> Present perfect vs. past tense

NEW VOCABULARY

assistant manager	department	Tennessee
bottom	Nashville	vice-president
clerk	salesperson	work *his* way up to the top
corporation	start at the bottom	

PREVIEWING THE STORY (optional)

Have students talk about the story title and/or illustrations. Introduce new vocabulary.

READING THE STORY

1. Have students read silently, or follow along silently as the story is read aloud by you, by one or more students, or on the tape.
2. Ask students if they have any questions; check understanding of vocabulary.
3. Check students' comprehension, using some or all of the following questions:

   a. How long has Louis been the store manager?
   b. How long was he a clerk?
   c. How long was he a cashier?
   d. How long was he an assistant manager?
   e. When did he become the manager?
   f. Why is everybody at the Big Value Supermarket proud of Louis?

   g. How long has Florence been the president?
   h. How long was she a salesperson in the Children's Clothing Department?
   i. How long was she the manager of the Women's Clothing Department?
   j. How long was she the store manager?
   k. What happened after that?
   l. When did she become the president?
   m. Why is everybody at the Jason Department Store in Nashville proud of Florence?

CHECK-UP

True, False, or Maybe?

1. False
2. True
3. Maybe
4. False
5. Maybe
6. True

IN YOUR OWN WORDS

1. Make sure students understand the instructions.
2. Have students do the activity as written homework, using a dictionary for any new words they wish to use.
3. Have students present and discuss what they have written, in pairs or as a class.

Text Pages 58–59

ON YOUR OWN: *It's Been a Long Time*

FOCUS

> Review of the present perfect tense

INTRODUCING THE MODEL

1. Have students look at the model illustration.
2. Set the scene: "Two old friends have just met on the street. They haven't seen each other in a long time."
3. Have students listen as you present the dialog or play the tape one or more times.
4. Ask students if they have any questions; check understanding of new vocabulary: *everything, taxi driver, saxophone, go fishing, Good idea, It's been a long time.*

   ### Language Note

   > *Good idea* is a reduced form of the expression *That's a good idea.*

5. Divide the class into pairs. Have students practice the dialog.
6. Call on one or two pairs of students to present the dialog.

SIDE BY SIDE EXERCISES

1. Divide the class into pairs. Have students role play the dialog using the guide on text page 59 and any vocabulary they wish.
2. Call on pairs of students to present the role play to the class without referring to the book.

WORKBOOK

Pages 52–54

Exercise Note

> Workbook p. 52: In this exercise, students use their imaginations as they pretend they're at their high school reunion. (It is common in the United States for high school classes to have gatherings of alumni every five or ten years after graduation.) Using the present perfect tense, students can make up answers to the questions with any vocabulary they wish. For oral practice, students can role play the people at the reunion.

EXPANSION ACTIVITY

Role Play: Let's Get Together

1. Write on the board:

A. How long has it been since you've _____?

B. It's been a long time. In fact, I haven't _____ { since / for } _____.

A. Would you like to get together and _____ this weekend?

B. That's a great idea.

---

2. Have pairs of students role play this friendly invitation, using any vocabulary they wish. For example:

    A. How long has it been since you've seen a movie?
    B. It's been a very long time. In fact, I haven't seen a movie for months.
    A. Would you like to get together and see a movie this weekend?
    B. That's a great idea.

WORKBOOK ANSWER KEY AND LISTENING SCRIPTS

Page 45   A.   HOW LONG?

1. I've had a toothache for
2. I've played the violin since
3. They've lived in London for
4. She's been interested in boys for
5. He's been an electrician since
6. We've known each other for
7. They've been in Europe since
8. I've had problems with my landlord for
9. She's liked science fiction books since
10. She's owned her own motorcycle since
11. There have been mice in my basement for

Page 46   B.   WHAT'S THE QUESTION?

1. How long has, wanted to be a doctor
2. How long has, owned her own car
3. How long have, been married
4. How long have, been interested in computer technology
5. How long has, worn glasses
6. How long have, been angry at each other
7. How long have, known how to knit
8. How long has, had a boyfriend
9. How long has, been a health club in town

Page 47   C.   SINCE WHEN?

1. I'm
   I've been
2. dances
   She's danced
3. We're
   We've been
4. It's
   It's been
5. I'm
   I've been
6. works
   He's worked
7. is
   It's been
8. argue
   They've argued
9. plays
   She's played
10. are
    We've been
11. have
    I've had
12. is
    He's been
13. hurt
    They've hurt

Page 49   D.   SCRAMBLED SENTENCES

1. Helen has had a headache since last night.
2. He's played the violin since he was a little boy.
3. I've been interested in Greek history since I visited Athens.
4. Paul and Sara/Sara and Paul have been engaged since they finished college.
5. We've known how to play the piano since we were very young.
6. You've wanted to be a professional musician since you were ten years old.

Page 50   F.   THEN AND NOW

1. go
   They've gone
   they, went
2. taught
   she teaches
   She's taught
3. I've lived
   I lived
4. He liked
   he likes
   He's liked
5. has
   visited
   visited
   visit
6. has
   He's had
   he had

Page 51   G.   LOOKING BACK

1. has Ralph been
   He's been a carpenter, 1970
2. was he
   He was an electrician, 14 years
3. has Mrs. Watson been
   She's been an English teacher, _____ years
4. was she
   She was a German teacher, 8 years
5. were your grandparents
   They were Republicans, 43 years
6. have they been
   They've been Democrats, 1973
7. has Maria worked
   She's worked at the bank, 1978
8. did she work
   She worked at the post office, 11 years
9. did Bob and Betsy live
   They lived in Toronto, 12 years
10. have they lived
    They've lived in Madrid, 1987

Page 54 I. LISTEN: *The Baker Family*

Listen to the story and fill in the information. Then use the information to answer the questions below.

Roger Baker is a math teacher. He's been a math teacher for fifteen years. Before that, he taught science.

His wife, Jane, is a professional violinist. She's been a professional violinist since she was twenty years old. She also composes music. She's already composed two symphonies.

The Bakers have three children: Jeff, Nancy, and Charlie. Jeff is interested in sports cars. He's wanted to be a professional sports car driver for the past five years. He's also interested in computers. He's been interested in computers since his family bought a small computer last year.

Nancy likes winter sports. She's liked winter sports since she was very young. She's a good skater, and she skis very well. She's known how to ski for ten years. She goes skiing whenever she can.

Charlie Baker is only six years old, but he's very interested in math. He already knows how to count to a hundred. He's known how to count to a hundred since he was three years old. He also plays the violin. He's played the violin for two years. When he grows up, he wants to be a math teacher like his father or a professional violinist like his mother.

1. How long has Mr. Baker been a math teacher?
2. What did he do before that?
3. How long has Mrs. Baker been a professional violinist?
4. How many symphonies has she composed?
5. How long has he been interested in computers?
6. How long has Nancy liked winter sports?

7. How long has she known how to ski?
8. How long has Charlie known how to count to a hundred?
9. How long has he played the violin?

Answers
1. 15 years
2. he taught science

3. she was 20 years old
4. 2

5. the past 5 years
6. his family bought a small computer last year

7. she was very young
8. 10 years

9. he was 3 years old
10. 2 years

1. He's been a math teacher for fifteen years.
2. He taught science.
3. She's been a professional violinist since she was twenty years old.
4. She's composed two symphonies.
5. He's wanted to be a professional sports car driver for the past five years.
6. He's been interested in computers since his family bought a small computer last year.
7. She's liked winter sports since she was very young.
8. She's known how to ski for ten years.
9. He's known how to count to a hundred since he was three years old.
10. He's played the violin for two years.

TEACHER'S NOTES

GRAMMAR

Present Perfect Continuous Tense

(I have)	I've	
(We have)	We've	
(You have)	You've	
(They have)	They've	been working.
(He has)	He's	
(She has)	She's	
(It has)	It's	

Have	I we you they	
Has	he she it	been working?

Yes,	I we you they	have.
	he she it	has.

Irregular Verbs

fly– flew –flown
drive–drove–driven
run– ran –run
sing– sang –sung

FUNCTIONS

Asking for and Reporting Information

What have you been doing?
  I've been *writing letters*.
How many *letters* have you *written*?
  I've already *written fifteen letters*.

How long have you been *waiting*?
  I've been *waiting* for *two hours*.
  I've been *waiting* since *twelve noon*.

What *are your neighbors* doing?
  They're arguing.
Have *they* been *arguing* for a long time?
  Yes, they have. *They've been arguing all day.*

Have you been *sleeping okay*?
Have you been *eating well* lately?

Where do you *live*?
How long have you been *living* there?
Have you *lived* anywhere else?
Where?
How long?

Have you ever *flown in an airplane*?

I'm going to *fly in an airplane tomorrow*, and I've never *flown in an airplane* before.

I've been *flying in airplanes for years*.

How are you feeling?
  I've been having problems with my _____.

We're having a problem with *our bedroom ceiling*.
  Oh? What's the problem?
It's leaking.

Tell me, _____.

Why?
How come?

Responding to Information

Really?

Indicating Understanding

I see.

Expressing Surprise-Disbelief

Fifteen letters?!

Sympathizing

I'm sorry to hear that.

Asking for Advice

Do you think that will help?

Offering Advice

I think you should _____.
I've been advising *all of them to* _____.

Describing Feelings-Emotions

I'm nervous.

Reassuring

Don't worry!

Believe me, there's nothing to be nervous about!

I'm sure you'll be feeling better soon.

Persuading

Believe me, . . .

Expressing Intention

I'll *take care of it* as soon as I can.

Greeting People

Hello.
  Hello. This is *Mrs. Banks*.
Yes, *Mrs. Banks*. What can I do for you?

Initiating a Topic

You look tired.
You look exhausted.

Expressing Gratitude

Thank you.
Thank you, *Doctor*.

You've been a great help.

Responding to Gratitude

It's been a pleasure.

NEW VOCABULARY

advise	job interview	review (v)
airplane	karate	ring (v)
all right	lately	run
as soon as	leak (v)	specialist
assemble	lie (v)	stand in line
baby-sitter	make noises	thank-you note
began (begin)	marathon	tickets
bother	mend	water heater
bridge	MTV	window washer
ceiling	officer	
Chemistry	parking ticket	a good night's sleep
Christmas present	peel	a great help
exhausted	phone (n)	believe me
furious	pick (v)	It's been a pleasure.
give *piano* lessons	pleasure	let me see
hallway	raise (n)	Yes, indeed.

LANGUAGE NOTES

The Present Perfect Continuous Tense

1. The present perfect continuous tense is formed with *has/have been* plus the present participle (*-ing* form) of the verb. *Have/has* is usually contracted in informal language.

    He's been studying since nine o'clock.
    I've been flying in airplanes for years.
    She's been having problems with her back.

2. Like the present perfect tense, the present perfect continuous tense is associated with a period of time beginning in the past and continuing up to the present. For example:

    We've been driving for seven hours.
    Robert has been ironing all day.

3. The present perfect continuous and the present perfect tenses are often interchangeable:

    How long $\left\{ \begin{array}{l} \textit{has he lived} \\ \textit{has he been living} \end{array} \right\}$ *in Toronto?*

    I've $\left\{ \begin{array}{l} \textit{studied} \\ \textit{been studying} \end{array} \right\}$ *English for a long time.*

4. Unlike the present perfect tense, the present perfect continuous cannot be used to describe an action or event which has ended or has been completed. Compare:

    I've been writing letters since ten o'clock this morning.
    I've already written fifteen letters.

5. As with other continuous tenses, certain verbs, when used as **stative verbs,** are not used in the present perfect continuous tense. These verbs include *know, like, be, own.*

Text Pages 62–63: *How Long Have You Been Waiting?*

FOCUS

> Introduction of the present perfect continuous tense

INTRODUCING THE MODEL

There are two model conversations. Introduce and practice each separately. For each model:

1. Have students look at the model illustration.
2. Set the scene:

   1st model: "Some people are waiting to see the doctor."
   2nd model: "Two people are talking about Henry."

3. Present the model.
4. Full-Class Choral Repetition.
5. Ask students if they have any questions; check understanding of new vocabulary:

   1st model: *have been waiting*
   2nd model: *has been working*

6. Group Choral Repetition.
7. Choral Conversation.
8. Call on one or two pairs of students to present the dialog.

   (For additional practice, do Choral Conversation in small groups or by rows.)

9. Form sentences with the words in the box at the top of the page and have students repeat chorally. For example:

   "I've been working."
   "We've been working."

10. Expand each model with further substitution practice. In the 1st model substitute *they, we, Mary*. For example:

    they:
    A. How long have they been waiting?
    B. They've been waiting for two hours.

    Similarly, in the 2nd model substitute *Bill and George, you, Jane*. For example:

    Bill and George:
    A. How long have Bill and George been working at the post office?
    B. They've been working at the post office since 1957.

SIDE BY SIDE EXERCISES

Examples

> 1. A. How long have you been feeling bad?
>   B. I've been feeling bad since yesterday morning.

2. A. How long has Nancy been playing the piano?
   B. She's been playing the piano for several years.

1. **Exercise 1:** Call on two students to present the dialog. Then do Choral Repetition and Choral Conversation Practice.
2. **Exercise 2:** Same as above.
3. **Exercises 3–12:**

   New vocabulary: 3. *phone, ring* (v)   11. *build, bridge*   12. *lie* (v)

   Either Full-Class Practice or Pair Practice.

WORKBOOK

Pages 55–56 (Exercise A)

EXPANSION ACTIVITIES

1. *Tell More about Situation 5*

   Have students look at the illustration for Exercise 5 and use their imaginations to tell more about Maria.

   a. Write these cues on the board:

   study hard
   do her homework every _____
   come to class on time
   speak English with _____
   go to (American/British/Canadian/. . .) movies
   _____
   _____
   _____

   b. Set the scene: "Maria is going to take a very important English exam soon. She's been trying to get ready for the exam."
   c. Have students use the cues on the board as well as ideas of their own to answer the question "What has Maria been doing?" For example:

   "She's been studying hard."
   "She's been doing her homework every day/week."
   "She's been coming to class on time."
   "She's been speaking English with other students."
   "She's been going to (American) movies."

d. Have students think of other things that Maria has been doing to improve her English. Have students pretend to be Maria and ask them:

> "What else have you been doing to get ready for the exam?"

Students might answer:

> "I've been reading (American) newspapers/books/magazines."
> "I've been listening to (British) radio programs."
> "I've been watching (American) TV programs."
> "I've been talking to my English teacher after class."
> "I've been listening to English language tapes."

2. Create a Story: Henry's Boring Life

Have students look at the illustration for the 2nd model in the book.

a. Write on the board:

> He _____.
>
> He's been _____ing every _____ {for the last / since} _____.

b. Set the scene: "Henry has been working at the post office since 1957. Henry is a very nice person, but his life is a little boring. Henry's life never changes. He's been doing the same things every day for many, many years."

c. Ask questions about Henry. Have students use the model on the board to tell about *Henry's boring life,* using any vocabulary they wish. For example:

> A. What does Henry eat for breakfast every morning?
> B. He eats an egg and a piece of bread. He's been eating an egg and a piece of bread for breakfast every morning for the last 20 years.

Suggestions for other questions:

> What time does Henry get up every morning?
> How does Henry get to work every day?
> What does Henry have for lunch every day?
> What does he do every evening after work?
> What time does he go to bed every night?
> Where does he go every Saturday night?
> When does he clean his apartment?
> What does he do every Sunday afternoon?
> Where does he go on vacation every year?

3. Role Play: I've Been VERY Busy

a. Write the following conversational model on the board:

> A. Hi, _____. How are you?
> B. Okay. And you?
> A. Fine, thanks. I haven't spoken to you for a few days. What's new?
> B. Well, . . . I've been VERY busy.
> A. Oh? What have you been doing?
> •
> •
> •

b. Divide the class into pairs. Have them create role plays based on the model on the board. Give one member of the pair a situation card (see below) as a cue for why he or she has been so busy. That person must tell about at least three things he or she has been doing.

You have a big test this Friday.
You've been _____ing.
    _____ing.
    _____ing.

You're having a big party this weekend.
You've been _____ing.
    _____ing.
    _____ing.

You're going on a vacation next week and
you've been very busy. You've been _____ing.
    _____ing.
    _____ing.

c. Have students *rehearse* their role plays, and then call on various pairs to present them to the class.

Text Page 64: *They've Been Arguing All Day*

FOCUS

> Present perfect continuous tense:
> - *Yes/no* questions and short answers
> - Contrast with the present continuous tense

INTRODUCING THE MODEL

1. Have students look at the model illustration.
2. Set the scene: "Two friends are talking. One of them is very upset about her noisy neighbors."
3. Present the model.
4. Full-Class Choral Repetition.
5. Ask students if they have any questions; check understanding of vocabulary.
6. Group Choral Repetition.
7. Choral Conversation.
8. Call on one or two pairs of students to present the dialog. Have some of the students substitute the alternative expressions (shown under the model) in place of *all day*.

   (For additional practice, do Choral Conversation in small groups or by rows.)

SIDE BY SIDE EXERCISES

Examples

> 1. A. What are you doing?
>   B. I'm studying.
>   A. Have you been studying for a long time?
>   B. Yes, I have. I've been studying all (morning).
>
> 2. A. What's Robert doing?
>   B. He's ironing.
>   A. Has he been ironing for a long time?
>   B. Yes, he has. He's been ironing all (afternoon).

1. **Exercise 1:** Call on two students to present the dialog. Then do Choral Repetition and Choral Conversation Practice.
2. **Exercise 2:** Same as above.
3. **Exercises 3–8:**

   > **New vocabulary:**   4. *stand in line, tickets*   7. *make noises*   8. *MTV*

   Either Full-Class Practice or Pair Practice.

4. **Exercise 9:** Have students use the model as a guide to create their own conversations, using vocabulary of their choice. Encourage students to use dictionaries to find new words they want to use. This exercise can be done orally in class or for written homework. If you assign it for homework, you should do one example in class to make sure students understand what's expected. Have students present their conversations in class the next day.

WORKBOOK

Pages 56–59 (Exercises B, C, D)

Exercise Note

Workbook p. 58: For additional oral practice with Exercise D, have students act out the conversations.

EXPANSION ACTIVITIES

1. *Negative Present Perfect Continuous: Practice with Visuals*

   Use *Side by Side* Picture Cards for verbs (18–41, 123–131, 136–139) or your own visuals.

   a. Write on the board:

   > A. $\begin{Bmatrix} \text{Has} \\ \text{Have} \end{Bmatrix}$ _____ been _____ing very long?
   >
   > B. No, _____ $\begin{Bmatrix} \text{hasn't} \\ \text{haven't} \end{Bmatrix}$ been _____ing long at all.
   >
   > In fact, _____ just started _____ing a few minutes ago.

   b. Point to a visual and call on a pair of students to create a conversation, using the model on the board. For example:

   (*Side by Side* Picture Card 18: *read*)
   A. Has he/Tom been reading very long?
   B. No, he hasn't been reading long at all.
   In fact, he just started reading a few minutes ago.

   (*Side by Side* Picture Card 28: *dance*)
   A. Have they been dancing very long?
   B. No, they haven't been dancing long at all.
   In fact, they just started dancing a few minutes ago.

2. *Tell More about Situation 5*

   a. Have students look at the illustration for Exercise 5 as you set the scene: "This is Ricky. He's been talking to his new girlfriend on the telephone for hours. He calls her every day. He's been calling her every day for weeks. I think Ricky is in love. His parents have been a little worried since he started going out with his new girlfriend. For example, he hasn't been eating very well. Also, he hasn't been seeing any of his old friends."

   b. Divide the class into small groups of three to five students. Have each group write 10 sentences about what Ricky has or hasn't been doing since he *fell in love*. Encourage students to use dictionaries.

   c. Have students from each group present their sentences to the class.

3. Role Play: *Waiting to See a Famous Person*

a. Write the following cues on the board:

> Who?
> How long?
> Why?

b. Divide the class into pairs. Student A is a TV reporter. Student B is waiting to see a famous person (a movie star/singer/athlete/politician) who is in the area.

c. Have the pairs create conversations based on the cues on the board. For example:

    A. Who are you waiting for?
    B. Elizabeth Taylor.
    A. How long have you been waiting?
    B. I've been waiting for more than two hours. But I think she's going to be here soon.
    A. Why are you waiting to see her?
    B. She's my favorite movie star!

Text Page 65

READING: *Apartment Problems*

FOCUS

Present perfect continuous tense

NEW VOCABULARY

ceiling	leak (v)
furious	peel
hallway	water heater

PREVIEWING THE STORY (optional)

Have students talk about the story title and/or illustration. Introduce new vocabulary.

READING THE STORY

1. Have students read silently, or follow along silently as the story is read aloud by you, by one or more students, or on the tape.
2. Ask students if they have any questions; check understanding of vocabulary.
3. Check students' comprehension, using some or all of the following questions.

   a. What's wrong with the bedroom ceiling?
   b. What's wrong with the refrigerator?
   c. What's wrong with the paint in the hallway?
   d. Why have they been taking cold showers?
   e. Why haven't they been sleeping at night?
   f. Who have they been calling every day?
   g. What has he been promising?
   h. Has he fixed anything yet?

CHECK-UP

Q & A

1. Call on a pair of students to present the model.
2. Have students work in pairs to create new dialogs.
3. Call on pairs to present their new dialogs to the class.

HOW ABOUT YOU?

Have students answer the question in pairs or as a class.

Text Pages 66–67: *No Wonder They're Tired!*

FOCUS

Contrast of the present perfect continuous and present perfect tenses

GETTING READY

Contrast the present perfect continuous and present perfect tenses.

1. Write on the board:

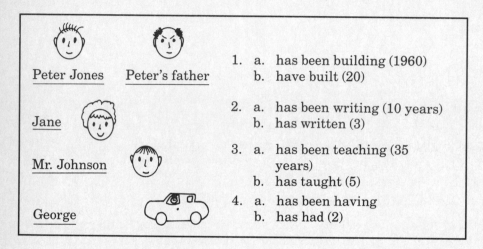

Peter Jones   Peter's father   1. a. has been building (1960)
                                      b. have built (20)

Jane   2. a. has been writing (10 years)
                                      b. has written (3)

Mr. Johnson   3. a. has been teaching (35 years)
                                      b. has taught (5)

George   4. a. has been having
                                      b. has had (2)

2. Have students listen as you read situations 1–4 below. Point to the appropriate cues on the board.

   1. Peter Jones and his father have been building houses since 1960. They've built twenty houses this year.
   2. Jane has been writing books for ten years. She's written three novels.
   3. Mr. Johnson has been teaching languages for thirty-five years. He's taught five different languages.
   4. George has been having accidents since he started driving. He's already had two accidents this year.

3. Check students' understanding of the two tenses.
4. Read each situation again and ask questions after each. For example:

   1. How long have Peter Jones and his father been building houses?
      How many houses have they built this year?

Note: In the "a" sentences in the box above, both the present perfect continuous and present perfect tenses can be used; in the "b" sentences, only the present perfect tense can be used.

INTRODUCING THE MODEL

There are two model conversations. Introduce and practice each separately. For each model:

1. Have students look at the model illustration.

2. Set the scene:

> 1st model: "Two roommates in an apartment are talking."
> 2nd model: "Two people are talking about Mary."

3. Present the model. (Note that the capitalized words indicate spoken emphasis.)
4. Full-Class Choral Repetition.
5. Ask students if they have any questions; check understanding of vocabulary.
6. Group Choral Repetition.
7. Choral Conversation.
8. Call on one or two pairs of students to present the dialog.
9. Introduce the new word *exhausted*. Have one or two pairs of students present the model again, using *exhausted* in place of *tired*.

    (For additional practice, do Choral Conversation in small groups or by rows.)

SIDE BY SIDE EXERCISES

Students can use any time expressions and numbers they wish in the exercises.

Examples

---

1. A. You look tired/exhausted. What have you been doing?
   B. I've been washing windows since (eight o'clock) this morning.
   A. Really? How many windows have you washed?
   B. Believe it or not, I've already washed (twenty) windows.
   A. (Twenty) windows?! NO WONDER you're tired/exhausted!

2. A. Dr. Anderson looks tired/exhausted. What has he been doing?
   B. He's been seeing patients since (nine o'clock) this morning.
   A. Really? How many patients has he seen?
   B. Believe it or not, he's already seen (eighteen) patients.
   A. (Eighteen) patients?! NO WONDER he's tired/exhausted!

---

1. **Exercise 1:** Call on two students to present the dialog. Then do Choral Repetition and Choral Conversation Practice.

2. **Exercise 2:** Same as above.

3. **Exercises 3–12:**

New vocabulary: 3. *give piano lessons*   4. *Christmas present*   5. *pick*   7. *mend*   9. *review* (v)   10. *thank-you note*   11. *job interview*

Culture Note

> Exercise 10: Thank-you notes are traditionally sent when one receives a gift such as a graduation or wedding gift, or after spending an overnight visit at someone's home.

Either Full-Class Practice or Pair Practice.

WORKBOOK

Pages 59–61 (Exercises E, F)

Exercise Note

Workbook p. 59:   In Exercise E, students complete the sentences with the present perfect continuous tense and any vocabulary they wish. Have students compare their answers.

EXPANSION ACTIVITIES

1. **Verb Review**

   With books closed, read each of the sentences below and have students complete it with an appropriate verb.

   a. How many photographs have you . . . ?   (taken)
   b. How many flowers has she . . . ?   (planted)
   c. How many letters have they . . . ?   (written) (read)
   d. How many movies have you . . . ?   (seen)
   e. How many socks has he . . . ?   (mended)
   f. How many interviews has your husband . . . ?   (gone to) (had)
   g. How many lessons has your piano teacher . . . ? (given)
   h. How many gifts has she . . . ?   (bought)

2. **Contrast of the Present Perfect Continuous and Present Perfect Tenses**

   a. Write on the board:

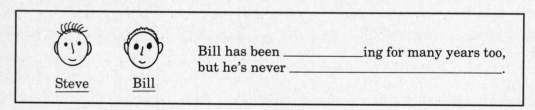

   Steve   Bill   Bill has been _____ing for many years too,
                    but he's never _____.

   b. Tell about *Steve* by reading the statements below. After each one, call on a student to make a contrasting statement about *Bill*. For example:

   > You: Steve has been driving for many years, and he's had a lot of accidents.

   > Student: Bill has been driving for many years too, but he's never had an accident.

   1. Steve has been studying French for many years, and he's traveled to France.
   2. Steve has been working in Washington for many years, and he's seen the President many times.
   3. Steve has been listening to jazz on the radio for many years, and he's gone to a lot of jazz concerts.
   4. Steve has been playing baseball for many years, and his team has won all their games.
   5. Steve has been studying the violin for many years, and he's missed a lot of lessons.
   6. Steve has been visiting New York for many years, and he's seen the Statue of Liberty several times.
   7. Steve has been going to movies for many years, and he's often fallen asleep in the movie theater.
   8. Steve has been going skiing every winter for many years, and he's broken his leg a few times.
   9. Steve has been going sailing every summer for many years, and he's gotten seasick a few times.

10. Steve has been cooking delicious meals for many years, and he's had several dinner parties.
11. Steve has been going camping every fall for many years, and he's hitchhiked a few times.
12. Steve has been studying European history for many years, and he's visited England twice.

Text Pages 68–69: *There's Nothing to Be Nervous About!*

FOCUS

Contrast of the present perfect and present perfect continuous tenses

INTRODUCING THE MODEL

1. Have students look at the model illustration.
2. Set the scene: "Two friends are talking. One of them is going on a trip tomorrow."
3. Present the model.
4. Full-Class Choral Repetition.
5. Ask students if they have any questions; check understanding of new vocabulary: *airplane, flown, for years, believe me, There's nothing to be nervous about.*
6. Group Choral Repetition.
7. Choral Conversation.
8. Call on one or two pairs of students to present the dialog.
9. Have one or two pairs of students present the model again, substituting *how come* for *why.*

   (For additional practice, do Choral Conversation in small groups or by rows.)

SIDE BY SIDE EXERCISES

Examples

1. A. I'm nervous.
   B. Why/How come?
   A. I'm going to buy a used car tomorrow, and I've never bought a used car before.
   B. Don't worry! I've been buying used cars for years. And believe me, there's nothing to be nervous about!

2. A. I'm nervous.
   B. Why/How come?
   A. I'm going to go to a job interview tomorrow, and I've never gone to a job interview before.
   B. Don't worry! I've been going to job interviews for years. And believe me, there's nothing to be nervous about!

1. **Exercise 1:** Call on two students to present the dialog. Then do Choral Repetition and Choral Conversation Practice.
2. **Exercise 2:** Same as above.
3. **Exercises 3–11:**

   New vocabulary: 3. *driven*   5. *karate*   6. *meeting*
   8. *audience, sung*   9. *run, marathon*   10. *ask for a raise*

Culture Notes

Exercise 9: Long-distance running and running in *marathons* for amateur athletes have become very popular in the United States since the 1970s. Some U.S. cities, such as Boston and New York, sponsor annual marathons.

Exercise 10: It is common for U.S. employees to give their workers regular salary increases. Employees may also ask for additional increases in salary if they feel they deserve more money for the work they do.

Either Full-Class Practice or Pair Practice.

After each exercise, ask students to tell about their own experiences; also have students ask each other. For example, after doing Exercise 2:

"Have you ever gone to a job interview?"
"Were you nervous?"
"What did you talk about?"

4. **Exercise 12:** Have students use the model as a guide to create their own conversations, using vocabulary of their choice. Encourage students to use dictionaries to find new words they want to use. This exercise can be done orally in class or for written homework. If you assign it for homework, you should do one example in class to make sure students understand what's expected. Have students present their conversations in class the next day.

HOW ABOUT YOU?

Have students answer the questions in pairs or as a class. Introduce the new expression *Have you ever.*

WORKBOOK

Pages 62–64

Exercise Notes

Workbook p. 63: Students use Exercise H as a model to write about a foreigner who is moving to their city. They use the present perfect and present perfect continuous tenses and any vocabulary they wish. Have students compare their answers.

Workbook p. 64: Students complete the conversation with any vocabulary they wish. Have students compare their answers.

EXPANSION ACTIVITIES

1. *Good Suggestions*

   a. Write the following conversational model on the board:

   > A. I've never _____ before. Do you have any suggestions?
   > B. Yes. You should _____, you should _____, and most of all you should _____.
   > A. Thanks. Those are good suggestions.

b. Have pairs of students talk about how to prepare for the situations on text pages 68 and 69, using the model on the board as a guide. For example:

> *Situation 2*
>
> A. I've never gone to a job interview before. Do you have any suggestions?
> B. Yes. You should prepare a resume, you should make a list of your qualifications, and most of all you should relax.
> A. Thanks. Those are good suggestions.

2. **Role Play: A Job Interview**

a. Write on the board:

> Where $\begin{Bmatrix} \text{have you} \\ \text{have you been} \end{Bmatrix}$ _____?
>
> Have you ever _____?
>
> How long $\begin{Bmatrix} \text{were} \\ \text{did} \end{Bmatrix}$ you _____?
>
> How long have you _____?

b. Divide the class into pairs. Have each pair write a 10–12 line dialog about a job interview. Have each pair choose a real or fictitious company where the interview is taking place. One student pretends to be the interviewer, and the other pretends to be the applicant. Have the interviewer use the question cues on the board to ask about the applicant's previous work experience. Encourage students to use dictionaries if they wish.

You can suggest that students begin:

> A. Good morning, (Mr./Mrs./Miss/Ms.) _____. How are you?
> B. Just fine, thank you. I understand you're looking for a _____, and I want to apply for the job.
> A. _____.
> B. _____.

Have students present their dialogs to the class.

Text Page 70

ON YOUR OWN: *At the Doctor's Office*

FOCUS

Review of the present perfect and present perfect continuous tenses

ON YOUR OWN ACTIVITY

1. Go over the dialog model with the students.

   a. Introduce the new vocabulary: *the first time, a good night's sleep, bother, began (begin), appetite, lately, let me see, indeed, advise, a great help, It's been a pleasure,* (at the bottom of the page) *specialist.*

   Language Note

   Well, . . . let me see is used when the speaker is trying to think of an answer to a question and needs some time to find an appropriate answer. It is a hesitation.

   b. Ask students if they have any questions.

2. Call on two of your better students to role play the conversation, using any vocabulary they wish.

3. Have students write the conversation for homework; students can use any vocabulary they wish to fill in the blanks.

4. In the next class, have pairs of students present their conversations to the class.

WORKBOOK

Page 65 (Exercise J)

READING: *It's Been a Long Day*

FOCUS

> - Present perfect tense
> - Present perfect continuous tense

NEW VOCABULARY

> | | |
> |---|---|
> | assemble | officer |
> | exhausted | parking ticket |

PREVIEWING THE STORY (optional)

Have students talk about the story title and/or illustrations. Introduce new vocabulary.

READING THE STORY

1. Have students read silently, or follow along silently as the story is read aloud by you, by one or more students, or on the tape.

2. Ask students if they have any questions; check understanding of vocabulary.

   Culture Note

   Parking is a problem in major U.S. cities. Public parking garages are expensive. Street parking is difficult to find. People have to put money into parking meters for street parking. Police officers give parking tickets to cars parked in illegal spaces and at meters that have run out of money.

3. Check students' comprehension, using some or all of the following questions:

   a. What has Mario been doing since 7 A.M.?
   b. How many cameras has he assembled?
   c. Has he ever assembled that many cameras in one day before?
   d. What does he have to do before he can go home?

   e. What has Judy been doing since 9 A.M.?
   f. How many letters has she typed?
   g. Has she ever typed that many letters in one day before?
   h. What does she have to do before she can go home?

   i. What have Officers Jackson and Parker been doing since 8 A.M.?
   j. How many parking tickets have they written?
   k. Have they ever written that many parking tickets in one day before?
   l. What do they have to do before they can go home?

CHECK-UP

Listening

Have students complete the exercises as you play the tape or read the following:

I. Listen and decide who is speaking.

1. What a day! All day the tenants have been complaining that nothing is working.   (a)
2. I'm very tired. I've given six lessons today.   (a)
3. It's been a long day. I've been selling tickets since 10 A.M.   (b)
4. I'm really tired. I've been watching them all day.   (b)
5. Thank you! You've been a wonderful audience!   (a)
6. I'm exhausted! I've been looking at paychecks since early this morning.   (b)

II. Listen and choose the word you hear.

1. She's gone to sleep.   (a)
2. I've never written so many letters in one day before.   (a)
3. I've been seeing patients all day.   (b)
4. What courses have you taken this year?   (a)
5. Is Henry giving blood?   (b)
6. Ben has driven all night.   (a)

IN YOUR OWN WORDS

1. Make sure students understand the instructions.
2. Have students do the activity as written homework, using a dictionary for any new words they wish to use.
3. Have students present and discuss what they have written, in pairs or as a class.

WORKBOOK

Check-Up Test: Pages 65–67

Page 55   A.   HOW LONG?

1. He's been sleeping since
2. They've been watching TV for
3. She's been making her own clothes since
4. We've been jogging for
5. He's been talking for
6. They've been dancing since
7. I've been teaching since
8. You've been lying here for
9. She's been studying since
10. We've been skating for
11. They've been doing aerobics for
12. He's been crying since

Page 56   B.   WHAT ARE THEY DOING?

1. is reading
   He's been reading
2. is working
   She's been working
3. are baking
   We've been baking
4. is riding
   He's been riding
5. are fighting
   You've been fighting
6. is writing
   She's been writing
7. is taking care of
   He's been taking care of
8. are complaining
   They've been complaining

Page 57   C.   SOUND IT OUT

1. his
2. teacher
3. Peter
4. will
5. evening
6. history
7. seeing
8. this
9. be

10. Peter will be seeing his history teacher this evening./This evening Peter will be seeing his history teacher./Will Peter be seeing his history teacher this evening?

11. isn't
12. he'll
13. this
14. busy
15. weekend
16. Steve
17. if
18. visit
19. be
20. If Steve isn't busy this weekend, he'll visit me./If Steve isn't busy, he'll visit me this weekend.

Page 58   D.   WHAT ARE THEY SAYING?

1. Has he been crying
   has, He's been crying
2. Have you been smoking
   have, I've been smoking
3. Have you been waiting
   haven't
4. haven't
   has she been working
   She's been working
5. Has it been raining
   has, It's been raining
6. Have you been living
   I haven't
7. Have they been studying
   have, They've been studying
8. Have you been wearing
   I haven't
9. Have you been playing
   haven't, I've been playing

Page 60   F.   WHAT'S HAPPENING?

1. They've been studying
   They've, studied
   They haven't studied

2. She's been painting
   She's, painted
   She hasn't painted
3. He's been reading
   He's, read
4. We've been eating
   We've, eaten
   We haven't eaten
5. He's been drinking
   He's, drunk
6. She's been swimming
   She's, swum
7. They've been playing
   They've, played
   haven't
8. I've been listening
   I've, listened
9. She's been typing
   She's, typed
10. They've been talking
    They've, talked
    they haven't talked
11. I've been meeting
    I've
    met
12. He's been giving
    He's, given

Page 62 G. A NEW LIFE

1. He's never lived in a big city
2. He's never taken English lessons
3. He's never shopped in American supermarkets
4. He's never eaten American food
5. . . . .

1. They've been living in a big city
2. They've been taking English lessons
3. They've been shopping in American supermarkets
4. They've been eating American food
5. . . . .

Page 65 J. LISTEN

Listen and fill in the missing words.

1. I've been seeing a lot of movies recently, but I haven't seen any that I've really liked. What good movies have you seen this month? Will you be seeing any movies this weekend?
2. Ted hasn't been driving very long, but he drives whenever he can. He's already driven downtown three times this week, and I think he's driving downtown again this afternoon.

3. Sheila has taken a lot of photographs of her children. She's been taking photographs of them for years. I think these two photographs are the best ones she's ever taken.
4. Mrs. Warren has given three piano lessons this morning, and she's giving another lesson in a few minutes. After that, she won't be giving any more lessons today.
5. Bobby isn't eating his dinner tonight because he's already eaten dessert. Bobby hasn't been eating very well since his grandmother sent him a large box of cookies last week.

Answers
1. seeing, movies, haven't seen
   have, seen this, Will
   be seeing, this weekend
2. hasn't been driving, drives
   can, He's, driven, this week
   he's driving
3. has taken, lot of, children, She's
   been taking, them, years, these two
   best, she's ever taken
4. has given three, morning
   she's giving, in, few minutes
   she won't be giving, today
5. isn't eating, he's, eaten
   hasn't been eating, since, sent
   him, cookies last

CHECK-UP TEST: *CHAPTERS 4–6*

Page 65 A.

1. have, gone
2. hasn't taken
3. haven't written
4. have, eaten
5. haven't paid
6. has, left

Page 66 B.

1. Has she worn
2. Have they gotten
3. Have you spoken
4. Has he seen
5. Have you, run
6. Has she, flown

Page 66 C.

1. It's been
2. We've been studying

3. He's had
4. They've been arguing
5. She's been sleeping
6. We've been
7. I've been baking
8. He's known

Page 67 D.

1. He's been working at the post office since
2. She's been married for
3. We've been waiting for
4. It's been raining since
5. I've wanted to be an actress since

Page 67 E.

1. He's owned
   he owned
2. I've been
   I was
3. They've had
   they had
4. She's liked
   she liked

Page 67 F.

Listen and fill in the missing words.

1. A. Timothy has been writing since he got up.
      He's already written more than ten pages.
      Who's he writing to?
   B. He's probably writing to his girlfriend. He
      hasn't written to her for weeks.
2. Mrs. Morgan has given three violin lessons
   this morning, but she won't be giving any
   more lessons this afternoon. She's been giving
   a lot of lessons recently, and she's feeling tired.

Answers

1.	has	14.	her
2.	been	15.	for
3.	writing	16.	has
4.	he	17.	given
5.	got	18.	morning
6.	He's	19.	won't
7.	written	20.	be
8.	writing	21.	giving
9.	to	22.	been
10.	writing	23.	giving
11.	his	24.	recently
12.	hasn't	25.	feeling
13.	written		

TEACHER'S NOTES

GRAMMAR

Infinitives
Gerunds

I	like can't stand started began continue	to work.
		working.

I	enjoy avoid considered keep on practice stopped quit	----------------
	I'm thinking about	swimming.

I learned I decided	to swim.

------------------	is my favorite way to relax.
Watching TV	

FUNCTIONS

Inquiring about Likes/Dislikes

Do you like to *watch TV?*

What do you like to *read?*

Expressing Likes

I enjoy *reading short stories.*
I enjoy *watching TV* very much.
I like to *read books about famous people.*

Watching TV is my favorite way to *relax.*

Expressing Dislikes

I can't stand *to talk on the telephone.*
I can't stand *talking on the telephone.*

I avoid *sitting in the sun* whenever I can.

Inquiring about Satisfaction

Are you enjoying the *party?*

Expressing Preference

I'd rather *be reading.*

Asking for Advice

I need some advice.

What do you think?

Do you think I'm making the right decision?

I have to decide *what to wear.*

Offering Advice

I don't mean to be critical, but I really think you should stop *smoking.*

I think *getting married* is a WONDERFUL idea!

Have you considered *wearing a suit and tie?*

Responding to Advice

That's a good idea.

I'll think about it.

Initiating a Topic

Guess what I've decided to do!

I have some good news!

Asking for and Reporting Information

Tell me, _____.

Can I ask you a question?

How about you?

I've never *swum* before.

I've decided to *get married.*

I considered *getting married YEARS ago,* but never did.

I've considered *wearing a sweater.*
I've been thinking about *wearing a sports jacket.*

I've been *eating junk food* for a long time.

How long have you been thinking about *getting married?*

How did you learn to *swim* so well?
I started to *swim* when I was *young,* and I've been *swimming* ever since.

Have you ever tried to *stop eating junk food* before?

Responding to Information

I'm glad you think so.

Focusing Attention

In fact, . . .

After all, . . .

Admitting

To tell you the truth, . . .

The truth is, . . .

Congratulating

That's GREAT!

Inquiring about Agreement

Don't you think so?

Expressing Agreement

You're right.

Absolutely!

Expressing Gratitude

Thank you.
Thanks.

I appreciate that.
That's very kind of you.
That's very nice of you.

Describing Feelings-Emotions

I envy you.

Hesitating

You know . . .

Attracting Attention

Harriet?

NEW VOCABULARY

appreciate
avoid
beard
box (v)
consider
continue
critical
decision
draw
engineering
enroll
envy (v)
ever since
figure skate (v)
go on a diet
go out of business
good news
gossip (v)
grow a beard
guess

habit
hate (v)
interrupt
junk food
keep on
make a decision
part
quit
rather
rest (n)
rude
sew
spinach
surf (v)
tease (v)
technical school
unhealthy
vegetarian

Absolutely!
after all
break a habit
can't stand
Don't you think so?
I appreciate that.
I don't mean to
I have some good news!
I think so.
I'll think about it.
It was nice meeting you.
Nice meeting you.
Not at all.
please excuse me
That's a good idea.
That's very kind of you.
That's very nice of you.
the truth is
to tell you the truth
What do you think?

Text Page 74: *My Favorite Way to Relax*

FOCUS

> - Introduction of:
>   *like to* _____
>   *enjoy* _____*ing*
> - Introduction of gerunds as subject of a sentence

GETTING READY

Introduce *like* with infinitives and *enjoy* with gerunds.

1. Write on the board:

   | like to | $\left\{\begin{array}{l}\text{read}\\\text{dance}\\\text{swim}\end{array}\right\}$ | enjoy | $\left\{\begin{array}{l}\text{reading}\\\text{dancing}\\\text{swimming}\end{array}\right\}$ |

2. Form sentences with the words on the board and have students repeat chorally. For example:

   "I like to read."   "(George) likes to dance."   "(Jane) likes to swim."
   "I enjoy reading."   "He enjoys dancing."   "She enjoys swimming."

3. Ask students questions in order to have them practice making statements about themselves, using these verbs. For example:

   | You: | What do you like to do? |
   | Student: | I like to swim. |

   | You: | What do you enjoy doing? |
   | Student: | I enjoy playing baseball. |

INTRODUCING THE MODEL

1. Have students look at the model illustration.
2. Set the scene: "Two friends are talking."
3. Present the model.
4. Full-Class Choral Repetition.
5. Ask students if they have any questions; check understanding of vocabulary.
6. Group Choral Repetition.
7. Choral Conversation.
8. Call on one or two pairs of students to present the dialog.
9. Expand the model with further substitution practice. Practice *she, he,* and *they* by substituting names of students in the class. For example:

   Does (Judy) like to watch TV?
   Yes. She enjoys watching TV very much.
   Watching TV is her favorite way to relax.

(For additional practice, do Choral Conversation in small groups or by rows.)

SIDE BY SIDE EXERCISES

Examples

> 1. A. Do you like to listen to music?
>   B. Yes. I enjoy listening to music very much.
>   Listening to music is my favorite way to relax.
> 2. A. Does Tom like to swim?
>   B. Yes. He enjoys swimming very much.
>   Swimming is his favorite way to relax.

1. **Exercise 1:** Call on two students to present the dialog. Then do Choral Repetition and Choral Conversation Practice.

2. **Exercise 2:** Same as above.

3. **Exercises 3–9:**

> **New vocabulary:** 7. *sew*

Either Full-Class Practice or Pair Practice. Whenever possible, after doing each exercise, ask students about their own likes and dislikes. For example:

> "Do you like to read?"
> "Do you enjoy dancing?"

WORKBOOK

Page 68

EXPANSION ACTIVITIES

1. Practice Gerunds and Infinitives: Places Around Your Town

  a. Write on the board:

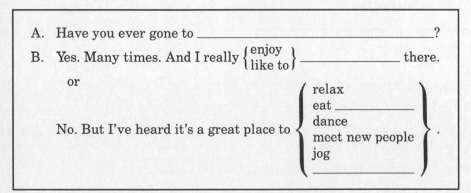

  b. Present the dialog with one of your students. You begin by asking about a place in your town such as a park, restaurant, cafe, or museum. For example:

> A. Have you ever gone to (The Europa Cafe)?
> B. Yes. Many times. And I really enjoy (eating) there.

A. Have you ever gone to (Central Park)?
B. No. But I've heard it's a great place to (jog).

c. Have students talk about other places around your town, using the model on the board.

2. *Practice Gerunds:* No _____ing

a. Write on the board:

A. Excuse me, but there's no _____ing in the _____!
B. Oh. I'm sorry. I didn't know that _____ing wasn't allowed.

---

b. Set the scene: "A man is in a department store. He's eating ice cream. A clerk walks over."
c. Present the dialog as follows:

A. Excuse me, but there's no eating in the store!
B. Oh. I'm sorry. I didn't know that eating wasn't allowed.

Check students' understanding of the new word *allowed*. Have students repeat chorally and individually. Then call on two students to present the dialog.

d. Write the situation cues below on cards or on the board:

1. bus
   driver → passenger

2. hospital
   employee → visitor

3. office
   boss → new employee

4. concert hall
   employee → listener

5. classroom
   teacher → student

6. airplane
   steward(ess) → passenger

e. Point to a cue and call on several pairs of students to create dialogs using the model on the board. Students should decide what isn't allowed. For example:

   cue 1

   A. Excuse me, but there's no (smoking) on the bus!
   B. Oh. I'm sorry. I didn't know that (smoking) wasn't allowed.

f. Ask students to think of other situations and make up dialogs for them.

3. *Student Interviews:* *Things I Like to Do*

a. Write the following on the board:

I like to _____.
I enjoy _____ing.
_____ing is my favorite way to relax.

---

b. On a separate piece of paper, have students complete these sentences with real information about themselves.
c. Collect the papers and distribute them randomly to students in the class.
d. Have students interview each other (Do you like to _____?/Do you enjoy _____ing?/ Is _____ing your favorite way to relax?) in order to match the correct person with the paper he or she is holding.

This can be done as a game, where the first person to identify the correct person wins.

Text Page 75

READING: *Enjoying Life*

FOCUS

> Gerunds

NEW VOCABULARY

> part

PREVIEWING THE STORY (optional)

Have students talk about the story title and/or illustrations. Introduce new vocabulary.

READING THE STORY

1. Have students read silently, or follow along silently as the story is read aloud by you, by one or more students, or on the tape.
2. Ask students if they have any questions; check understanding of vocabulary.
3. Check students' comprehension, using some or all of the following questions:

    a. What does Howard enjoy doing?
    b. Where does he like to read?

    c. What does Patty enjoy doing?
    d. Where does she like to sing?

    e. What does Brenda enjoy doing?
    f. Where does she like to watch TV?

    g. What does Tom enjoy doing?
    h. Who does Tom like to talk about politics with?

CHECK-UP

Q & A

1. Call on a pair of students to present the model.
2. Have students work in pairs to create new dialogs.
3. Call on pairs to present their new dialogs to the class.

Text Page 76: *He Can't Stand to Travel by Plane*

FOCUS

> - *like* $\left\{ \begin{array}{l} to\ \underline{\hspace{2cm}} \\ \underline{\hspace{2cm}}ing \end{array} \right\}$
>
> - *can't stand* $\left\{ \begin{array}{l} to\ \underline{\hspace{2cm}} \\ \underline{\hspace{2cm}}ing \end{array} \right\}$
>
> - *avoid* $\underline{\hspace{2cm}}ing$

GETTING READY

Introduce *like, can't stand,* and *avoid.*

1. Write on the board:

2. Tell the story below one or two times. Point to the appropriate verb on the board as you tell each part of the story.

    a. Ronald *likes to study* languages.
    b. And he *likes meeting* people from other countries.
    c. Unfortunately, he *can't stand to travel.*
    d. He *can't stand riding* in airplanes.
    e. And he *hates to take* trains.
    f. He also *hates driving* long distances.
    g. It's too bad that Ronald *avoids traveling.* I think he could meet a lot of nice people.

3. Point to each verb on the board as you say the sentence again; have students repeat chorally.

INTRODUCING THE MODEL

In this model conversation, the verbs *like* and *can't stand* can be used with the infinitives *to travel* or the gerund *traveling.* Present the model first with the infinitive; then present it again with the gerund.

1. Have students look at the model illustration.
2. Set the scene: "Two people are talking about Ronald."
3. Present the model.
4. Full-Class Choral Repetition.

5. Ask students if they have any questions; check understanding of new vocabulary: *can't stand, avoid.*
6. Group Choral Repetition.
7. Choral Conversation.
8. Call on several pairs of students to present the dialog.
9. Introduce the expression *hate to* _____ /hate _____*ing.*

   Call on pairs of students to present the dialog again using *hate* in place of *can't stand.*

   (For additional practice, do Choral Conversation in small groups or by rows.)

SIDE BY SIDE EXERCISES

Examples

> 1. A. Does Sally like to do/like doing her homework?
>   B. No. She can't stand to do/can't stand doing her homework.
>   She avoids doing her homework whenever she can.
>
> 2. A. Do Mr. and Mrs. Simon like to drive/like driving downtown?
>   B. No. They can't stand to drive/can't stand driving downtown.
>   They avoid driving downtown whenever they can.

1. **Exercise 1:** Call on two students to present the dialog. Then do Choral Repetition and Choral Conversation Practice.
2. **Exercise 2:** Same as above.
3. **Exercises 3–9:**

> **New vocabulary:** 6. *spinach*

Culture Note

> Exercise 6: People in the United States often joke about the fact that spinach is a nutritious food that children sometimes refuse to eat.

Either Full-Class Practice or Pair Practice.

HOW ABOUT YOU?

Have students answer the questions in pairs or as a class.

WORKBOOK

Page 69 (Exercise B)

Exercise Note

> Workbook p. 69: Students complete the sentences in Exercise B with any vocabulary they wish. Have students compare their answers.

EXPANSION ACTIVITIES

1. *Role Play:*   *A Difficult Customer*

    a. Put the following conversational model on the board or on a large poster, or distribute copies to your students:

    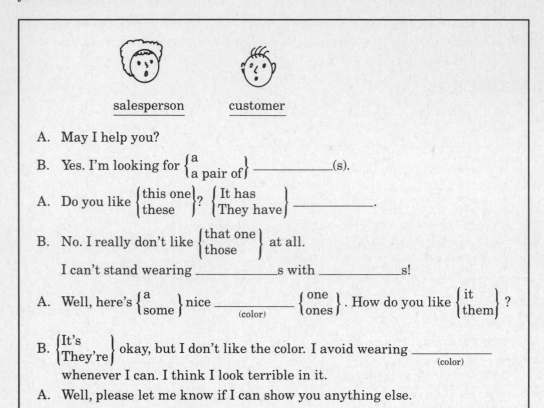

    salesperson   customer

    A. May I help you?

    B. Yes. I'm looking for { a / a pair of } _____(s).

    A. Do you like { this one / these }? { It has / They have } _____.

    B. No. I really don't like { that one / those } at all.

    I can't stand wearing _____s with _____s!

    A. Well, here's { a / some } nice _____ (color) { one / ones }. How do you like { it / them } ?

    B. { It's / They're } okay, but I don't like the color. I avoid wearing _____ (color) whenever I can. I think I look terrible in it.

    A. Well, please let me know if I can show you anything else.

    b. Review articles of clothing, using your own visuals.

    c. Write the additional vocabulary below on the board. Introduce these words, using your own visuals (for example, magazine pictures):

long sleeves	button
short sleeves	zipper
high heels	pocket
low heels	fur collar

    d. Set the scene: "A salesperson and a customer are talking. The customer doesn't like anything in the store."

    e. Present the dialog, using the examples below. Have students refer to the conversational model as you read each line. For example:

    A. May I help you?
    B. Yes. I'm looking for a coat.
    A. Do you like this one? It has a fur collar.
    B. No. I really don't like that one at all. I can't stand wearing coats with fur collars!

A. Well, here's a nice blue one. How do you like it?
B. It's okay, but I don't like the color. I avoid wearing blue whenever I can. I think I look terrible in it.
A. Well, please let me know if I can show you anything else.

A. May I help you?
B. Yes. I'm looking for a pair of shoes.
A. Do you like these? They have high heels.
B. No. I really don't like those at all. I can't stand wearing shoes with high heels!
A. Well, here are some nice green ones. How do you like them?
B. They're okay, but I don't like the color. I avoid wearing green whenever I can. I think I look terrible in it.
A. Well, please let me know if I can show you anything else.

f. Role play each of these conversations with a student. You take the part of the *salesperson*.

g. Do Choral Repetition if you feel your students need the practice.

h. Call on pairs of students to create new conversations based on the model. Students can refer to the new vocabulary on the board and use any article of clothing and any color they wish. Encourage students to have fun portraying the *difficult customer*.

2. *Students Talk about Themselves*

a. Write the following verbs and conversational model on the board:

watch	listen to	do	talk about	read
eat	practice	play	talk to	go to

A. Do you { like to / like / enjoy } _____ ?
B. Yes. _____.
    or
    No. I can't stand _____.
A. Why do you enjoy it?/Why don't you enjoy it?
B. Because _____.

b. Have pairs of students create conversations based on the model on the board and any of the verbs. For example:

A. Do you enjoy talking about world politics?
B. Yes. I like it a lot.
A. Why do you enjoy it?
B. Because I think it's interesting to hear other people's opinions.

A. Do you like to practice the piano?
B. No. I can't stand practicing the piano.
A. Why don't you enjoy it?
B. Because it's boring, and it takes a lot of time.

Text Page 77

READING: *Bad Habits*

FOCUS

> Gerunds

NEW VOCABULARY

break a habit	keep on
gossip (v)	rude
habit	unhealthy
interrupt	

PREVIEWING THE STORY (optional)

Have students talk about the story title and/or illustrations. Introduce new vocabulary.

READING THE STORY

1. Have students read silently, or follow along silently as the story is read aloud by you, by one or more students, or on the tape.
2. Ask students if they have any questions; check understanding of vocabulary.

   Culture Note

   Smoking is a big issue in the United States. Laws prohibit smoking in many public buildings, restaurants, and on airplanes. Smokers are under great pressure to quit.

3. Check students' comprehension, using some or all of the following questions:

   a. What do Harriet's friends tell her?
   b. Why?
   c. Has Harriet stopped smoking?
   d. Why can't she stop?

   e. What do Vincent's friends tell him?
   f. Why?
   g. Has Vincent stopped gossiping?
   h. Why can't he stop?

   i. What does Jennifer's mother tell her?
   j. Why?
   k. Has Jennifer stopped interrupting people while they're talking?
   l. Why can't she stop?

   m. What does Walter's wife tell him?
   n. Why?
   o. Has Walter stopped talking about business?
   p. Why can't he stop?

CHECK-UP

Q & A

1. Call on a pair of students to present the model.
2. Have students work in pairs to create new dialogs.
3. Call on pairs to present their new dialogs to the class.

HOW ABOUT YOU?

Have students do the activity in pairs or as a class.

Text Pages 78–79: *How Did You Learn to Swim So Well?*

FOCUS

- Introduction of:

  $start \begin{Bmatrix} to \text{\underline{\hspace{2cm}}} \\ \text{\underline{\hspace{2cm}}} ing \end{Bmatrix}$

  learn to _____

  practice _____ ing

- Review of tenses

GETTING READY

Introduce *start, learn,* and *practice.*

1. Write on the board:

    learned to _____
    started to _____
    started _____ ing
    practice _____ ing

2. Tell the story below about *Bruno* one or two times. Point to the appropriate verb on the board as you tell each part of the story.

    a. Bruno *learned to swim* at the beach a long time ago.
    b. His family *started to go* to the beach every summer when he was five years old.
    c. And that's when Bruno *started swimming.*
    d. Now he *practices swimming* in the swimming pool at school whenever he can.

3. Point to each verb on the board as you say each sentence again; have students repeat chorally.

INTRODUCING THE MODEL

1. Have students look at the model illustration.
2. Set the scene: "Two classmates are talking."
3. Present the model. In line 2, first say the sentence with *started to swim.* Present the sentence again, using *started swimming.*
4. Full-Class Choral Repetition.
5. Ask students if they have any questions; check understanding of new vocabulary: *ever since, envy, Not at all.*
6. Group Choral Repetition.
7. Choral Conversation.
8. Call on two pairs of students to present the dialog. Have one pair use *started to swim* and have the other use *started swimming.*
9. Introduce the new expressions *I appreciate that, That's very kind of you, That's very nice of you.* Call on pairs of students to present the model again, using these expressions in place of *Thank you.*

    (For additional practice, do Choral Conversation in small groups or by rows.)

SIDE BY SIDE EXERCISES

Examples

1. A. How did you learn to draw so well?
   B. Well, I started drawing/started to draw when I was young, and I've been drawing ever since.
   A. I envy you. I've never drawn before.
   B. I'll be glad to teach you how.
   A. Thank you. (I appreciate that./That's very kind of you./That's very nice of you.) But isn't drawing very difficult?
   B. Not at all. After you practice drawing a few times, you'll probably draw as well as I do.

2. A. How did you learn to ski so well?
   B. Well, I started skiing/started to ski when I was young, and I've been skiing ever since.
   A. I envy you. I've never skied before.
   B. I'll be glad to teach you how.
   A. Thank you. (I appreciate that./That's very kind of you./That's very nice of you.) But isn't skiing very difficult?
   B. Not at all. After you practice skiing a few times, you'll probably ski as well as I do.

1. **Exercise 1:** Introduce the new verb *draw–drew–drawn*. Call on two students to present the dialog. Then do Choral Repetition and Choral Conversation Practice.

2. **Exercise 2:** Same as above.

3. **Exercises 3–7:**

   > **New vocabulary:**   3. *figure skate*   4. *surf* (v)   7. *box*

   Either Full-Class Practice or Pair Practice.

4. **Exercise 8:** Have students use the model as a guide to create their own conversations, using vocabulary of their choice. Encourage students to use dictionaries to find new words they want to use. This exercise can be done orally in class or for written homework. If you assign it for homework, you should do one example in class to make sure students understand what's expected. Have students present their conversations in class the next day.

WORKBOOK

Pages 69–70 (Exercises C, D)

Exercise Note

Workbook p. 70: For Exercise D, call on students to read their paragraphs aloud . . . with expression.

EXPANSION ACTIVITIES

1. *Students Talk about Themselves*

   a. Write on the board:

   > I can _____ very well.

b. Call on students to tell about something they're good at. For example:

"I can play tennis well./I can skate very well."

c. Ask students the following questions:

When did you start to _____? (or) When did you start _____ing?
Is _____ing easy or difficult?
Why?/Why not?
How often do you practice _____ing?

You may wish to have pairs of students interview each other, using these questions. Have students then report back to the class about the person they interviewed.

2. Role Play: *Welcome to School*

a. Write on the board:

A. Welcome to _____ School! We're very glad you're going to be studying here with us. Do you have any questions?
B. Yes. What will we be learning first?
A. First, we'll learn to _____, and we'll practice _____.
B. And what will we be learning after that?
A. Next, we'll practice _____ and we'll learn how to _____.
B. And when will we start studying _____?
A. _____.
B. Oh, that'll be great! I'm really looking forward to starting school.

---

b. Divide the class into pairs. Have each pair choose or make up the name of a training school. For example:

The (Speedy) Secretarial School
The (Ace) Driving School
The (Chen) Cooking School
(Charlie's) Auto Repair School
The (Century) Computer Programming School
The (Ajax) Accounting School

Have each pair create a role play about the school, using the model on the board. Speaker A pretends to be the director or a teacher. Speaker B is a new student. Have students use dictionaries to find new vocabulary for skills one might learn at that school.

c. Have students present their role plays to the class. For example:

A. Welcome to (the Speedy Secretarial School)! We're very glad you're going to be studying here with us. Do you have any questions?
B. Yes. What will we be learning first?
A. First we'll learn to (type) and we'll practice (typing business letters).
B. And what will we be learning after that?
A. Next, we'll practice (using a dictaphone), and we'll learn how to (take dictation).
B. And when will we start studying (accounting)?
A. (We'll start studying accounting in a few weeks.)
B. Oh, that'll be great! I'm really looking forward to starting school.

Text Pages 80–81: *Guess What I've Decided to Do!*

FOCUS

Introduction of:

decide to _____
consider _____*ing*
think about _____*ing*

GETTING READY

Introduce the new expressions *consider* _____*ing*, *think about* _____*ing*, and *decide to* _____.

1. Write on the board:

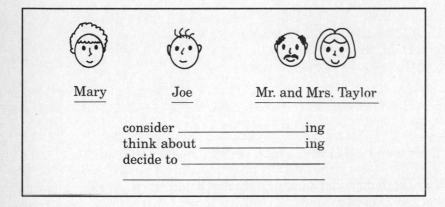

Mary   Joe   Mr. and Mrs. Taylor

consider _____ing
think about _____ing
decide to _____
_____

2. Have students listen for the new verbs as you read about the people on the board one or more times:

    a. "Mary recently moved into a new apartment. She's *considering buying* a new TV. She saw a color TV in a store downtown, and she's *thinking about buying* it."

    b. "Joe graduated from high school recently. He's looking for a job. He *considered going* to college. And for a while he *was thinking about* visiting some schools. But he's *decided to work* for a few years first."

    c. "Mr. and Mrs. Taylor are going to retire next year. They're *considering moving* after that. They're *thinking about selling* their house in the suburbs and *buying* an apartment in the city. They aren't sure what they'll do."

3. Check students' understanding of the new verbs by asking questions about each person. Have students retell as much of each story as they can. For example, after telling about Mary you can ask:

    "What did Mary do recently?"
    "What's she considering doing?"

INTRODUCING THE MODEL

1. Have students look at the model illustration.
2. Set the scene: "Two friends are talking."
3. Present the model.

4. Full-Class Choral Repetition.

5. Ask students if they have any questions; check understanding of new vocabulary: *guess, consider, make a decision, Absolutely!*

6. Group Choral Repetition.

7. Choral Conversation.

8. Call on one or two pairs of students to present the dialog.

   (For additional practice, do Choral Conversation in small groups or by rows.)

SIDE BY SIDE EXERCISES

Examples

1. A. Guess what I've decided to do!
   B. What?
   A. I've decided to move to Chicago.
   B. You HAVE? That's GREAT! Tell me, how long have you been thinking about moving to Chicago?
   A. For a long time, actually. I considered moving to Chicago YEARS ago, but never did. Do you think I'm making the right decision?
   B. Absolutely! I think moving to Chicago is a WONDERFUL idea!
   A. I'm glad you think so.

2. A. Guess what I've decided to do!
   B. What?
   A. I've decided to buy a new car.
   B. You HAVE? That's GREAT! Tell me, how long have you been thinking about buying a new car?
   A. For a long time, actually. I considered buying a new car YEARS ago, but never did. Do you think I'm making the right decision?
   B. Absolutely! I think buying a new car is a WONDERFUL idea!
   A. I'm glad you think so.

1. **Exercise 1:** Call on two students to present the dialog. Then do Choral Repetition and Choral Conversation Practice.

2. **Exercises 2–8:**

   > **New vocabulary:**   5. *grow (grew, grown) a beard*   8. *vegetarian*

   Either Full-Class Practice or Pair Practice.

3. **Exercise 9:** Have students use the model as a guide to create their own conversations, using vocabulary of their choice. (They can use any names, places, and activities they wish). Encourage students to use dictionaries to find new words they want to use. This exercise can be done orally in class or for written homework. If you assign it for homework, you should do one example in class to make sure students understand what's expected. Have students present their conversations in class the next day.

WORKBOOK

Page 71

Exercise Note

Workbook p. 71: In this exercise, students complete parts of a telephone conversation by using gerunds and infinitives. For additional oral practice, have students act out the conversation.

EXPANSION ACTIVITIES

1. *Students Talk about Themselves*

   a. Write on the board:

A. What are you going to do after you finish {this class / high school}?

B. I'm not really sure. I've been {thinking about / considering} _____ing.

A. I've {thought about / considered} that, too.

And I've also been {thinking about / considering} _____ing.

   or

But I've decided to _____.

---

   b. Have pairs of students create conversations about their own future plans. Encourage students to vary and expand the dialog in any way they wish. For example:

   A. What are you going to do after you finish this class?
   B. I'm not really sure. I've been thinking about taking another English course.
   A. I've thought about that, too. And I've also considered taking a typing course.

   A. What are you going to do after you finish high school?
   B. I'm not really sure. I've been considering going to auto mechanics school.
   A. I've considered that, too. But I've decided to go to college.

2. *Role Play: Giving Advice*

   a. Write the following conversational model on the board:

A. I'm having a problem with my _____.
B. What's the matter?
A. _____.
B. That's too bad. {Have you considered _____ing? / Have you thought about _____ing?}
A. That's a good idea.

---

   b. Divide the class into pairs. Give one member of the pair a cue card with one of the following:

car	cat	supervisor
bicycle	roof	English teacher
son	feet	girlfriend
daughter	back	boyfriend
dog	boss	kitchen sink

   (or any other topic of your choice)

c. Have the pairs create role plays based on the cue cards and the conversational model on the board.

d. Call on pairs to present their role plays to the class. For example:

        A. I'm having a problem with my back.

        B. What's the matter?

        A. It hurts after I sit at my desk all day.

        B. That's too bad. Have you thought about doing back exercises?

        A. That's a good idea.

Text Page 82

ON YOUR OWN: *I Have Some Good News!*

FOCUS

- Review of *start to* _____
- Introduction of new expressions:

    $begin \begin{cases} to\underline{\hspace{2cm}} \\ \underline{\hspace{2cm}}ing \end{cases}$

    $continue \begin{cases} to\underline{\hspace{2cm}} \\ \underline{\hspace{2cm}}ing \end{cases}$

    keep on _____ *ing*

    stop _____ *ing*

    quit _____ *ing*

GETTING READY

Introduce the new verbs in this lesson.

1. Write on the board:

    1. Roger $\begin{cases} \text{started to} \underline{\hspace{2cm}} \\ \text{started} \underline{\hspace{2cm}}ing \\ \text{began to} \underline{\hspace{2cm}} \\ \text{began} \underline{\hspace{2cm}}ing \end{cases}$ several years ago.

    2. He has $\begin{cases} \text{kept on} \underline{\hspace{2cm}}ing \\ \text{continued to} \underline{\hspace{2cm}} \\ \text{continued} \underline{\hspace{2cm}}ing \end{cases}$ every day since then.

    3. He says he'll never $\begin{cases} \text{stop} \underline{\hspace{2cm}}ing \\ \text{quit} \underline{\hspace{2cm}}ing \end{cases}$.

2. Tell about Roger; have students repeat chorally:

    1. Roger started riding his bicycle to work several years ago.
    2. He has kept on riding his bicycle to work every day since then.
    3. He says he'll never stop riding his bicycle to work.

3. Call out the other verb forms and have students create sentences about Roger using those verbs. For example, the other forms for number 1 are *started to ride, began to ride, began riding*. Example:

    You: began riding
    Student: Roger began riding his bicycle to work several years ago.

INTRODUCING THE MODEL

Go over the model dialog; introduce the new vocabulary: *good, news, begun, I hope so, after all, the rest of.*

SIDE BY SIDE EXERCISES

1. **Exercise 1:** Introduce the new expression *junk food*. Call on two students to present the dialog. Then do Choral Repetition and Choral Conversation Practice.

2. **Exercises 2–3:**

> | New vocabulary: | 2. *tease* |
> |---|---|

Culture Note

Exercise 1: *Junk food* refers to packaged snack foods such as soft drinks, potato chips, and candy.

3. **Exercise 4:** Have students use the model as a guide to create their own conversations, using vocabulary of their choice. Encourage students to use dictionaries to find new words they want to use. This exercise can be done orally in class or for written homework. If you assign it for homework, you should do one example in class to make sure students understand what's expected. Have students present their conversations in class the next day.

WORKBOOK

Pages 72–75

EXPANSION ACTIVITIES

1. Vocabulary Review

a. Write the three sentences from **Getting Ready** on the board again, omitting the name *Roger*.

> 1. _____ { started to _____ / began _____ ing } several years ago.
>
> 2. _____ has { kept on _____ ing / continued to _____ / continued _____ ing } every day since then.
>
> 3. _____ says _____'ll never { stop / quit } _____ ing .

b. Give students cues, such as those below, and have students make up sentences according to the models on the board. (Also have students think of their cues.)

> Janet/drink coffee
> Mrs. Rogers/do exercises
> The Goody Candy Company/make candy
> Bob/smoke cigars
> _____/_____

Example:

1. Janet started to drink coffee several years ago.
2. She has continued to drink coffee every day since then.
3. She says she'll never quit drinking coffee.

2. Role Play: Why Didn't You Complain?

a. Write on the board:

A. How did you like the $\begin{Bmatrix} \text{concert} \\ \text{movie} \\ \text{play} \\ \underline{\hspace{1cm}}\text{ game} \\ \underline{\hspace{1.5cm}} \end{Bmatrix}$ last night?

B. We didn't have a very good time. There were some people sitting near us who _____ the whole time.

A. What a shame! Why didn't you complain to somebody?

B. Well, we thought they were going to $\begin{Bmatrix} \text{stop} \\ \text{quit} \end{Bmatrix}$_____,

but they didn't. They $\begin{Bmatrix} \text{started} \\ \text{began} \end{Bmatrix}$_____ when we got there,

and they $\begin{Bmatrix} \text{kept on} \\ \text{continued} \end{Bmatrix}$_____ during the whole _____.

---

b. Have pairs of students create conversations, using any vocabulary they wish. For example:

A. How did you like the movie last night?
B. We didn't have a very good time. There were some people sitting near us who talked the whole time.
A. What a shame! Why didn't you complain to somebody?
B. Well, we thought they were going to stop talking, but they didn't. They started to talk when we got there, and they continued talking during the whole movie.

3. What Should You Do?

a. Write the following on the board:

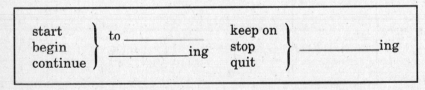

b. Ask questions such as the following and have students answer, using appropriate verbs from the board. For example:

1. You're driving along a street, and you see a red light. What should you do?
        (You should stop driving.)

2. You're driving along a street, and you see a green traffic light. What should you do?
        (You should continue to drive.)
        (You should continue driving.)
        (You should keep on driving.)

3. You've been eating dinner, and you're feeling full. What should you do?
        (You should stop eating.)
        (You should quit eating.)

4. You've just started to eat dinner, and you're still hungry. What should you do?
        (You should continue eating.)
        (You should continue to eat.)
        (You should keep on eating.)

5. You have an exam tomorrow, and you haven't opened a book yet. What should you do?
   (You should start to study.)
   (You should start studying.)
   (You should quit watching TV.)
   (You should stop talking on the telephone.)

c. Divide the class into small groups. Have each group think of five questions to ask the other groups.

Text Pages 83–85

READING: *Important Decisions*

FOCUS

> - Gerunds
> - Infinitives

NEW VOCABULARY

> engineering
> technical school
> go out of business

PREVIEWING THE STORY (optional)

Have students talk about the story title and/or illustrations. Introduce new vocabulary.

READING THE STORY

1. Have students read silently, or follow along silently as the story is read aloud by you, by one or more students, or on the tape.
2. Ask students if they have any questions; check understanding of vocabulary.
3. Check students' comprehension, using some or all of the following questions:

   a. Why did Jim have to make an important decision recently?
   b. What did he consider doing first?
   c. Then what did he think about doing?
   d. What did he finally decide to do?
   e. How does Jim feel about his decision?

   f. Why did Lana have to make an important decision recently?
   g. What did she consider doing first?
   h. Then what did she think about doing?
   i. What did she finally decide to do?
   j. How does Lana feel about her decision?

   k. Why did Nick have to make an important decision recently?
   l. What did he consider doing first?
   m. Then what did he think about doing?
   n. What did he finally decide to do?
   o. How does Nick feel about his decision?

   p. Why did Maria have to make an important decision recently?
   q. What did she consider doing first?
   r. Then what did she think about doing?
   s. What did she finally decide to do?
   t. How does Maria feel about her decision?

CHECK-UP

True, False, or Maybe?

1.	True	6.	False
2.	Maybe	7.	Maybe
3.	True	8.	Maybe
4.	False	9.	False
5.	Maybe	10.	True

Q & A

1. Call on a pair of students to present the model.
2. Have students work in pairs to create new dialogs.
3. Call on pairs to present their new dialogs to the class.

Choose

I.	1.	b
	2.	b
	3.	a
	4.	b
	5.	b
	6.	a

II.	1.	b
	2.	b
	3.	a
	4.	b
	5.	a
	6.	a

Listening

Have students complete the exercises as you play the tape or read the following:

Listen and choose the best answer.

1. A. I avoid driving downtown whenever I can.
   B. Me, too. (b)

2. A. I've decided to sell my car.
   B. Your beautiful car? (b)

3. A. Please try to quit biting your nails.
   B. Okay, Mom. (a)

4. A. We're thinking about moving to California.
   B. Oh. That's interesting. (b)

5. A. I've been considering getting married for a long time.
   B. Oh, really? I didn't know that. (b)

6. A. Don't stop practicing!
   B. Okay. (a)

IN YOUR OWN WORDS

1. Make sure students understand the instructions.
2. Have students do the activity as written homework, using a dictionary for any new words they wish to use.
3. Have students present and discuss what they have written, in pairs or as a class.

**Page 68 A. WHAT DO THEY
{ENJOY DOING
LIKE TO DO? }?**

1. going
2. likes to
   lifting
3. enjoys
4. like to, swimming
5. enjoy
6. like
7. like to, giving
8. enjoy
9. likes to, jogging
10. like to, going to parties
11. enjoy
12. likes to, eating
13. cleaning
14. like to, going
15. getting up
16. like to

6. to tease/teasing
   teasing
   crying
   teasing
7. to study/studying
   studying
   studying
8. driving
   to drive/driving, Driving
9. to dress/dressing
   dressing
10. stepping
    stepping
11. watching
    watching
    having
12. going
    to go/going
    going

**Page 69 C. MY ENERGETIC
GRANDMOTHER**

1. playing
2. to play
3. play
4. . . . .
5. . . . .
6. . . . .
7. . . . .

Page 74 G. LISTEN

Listen and put a circle around the correct answer.

1. My brother-in-law Tom really enjoys . . .
2. Whenever possible, my husband and I try to avoid . . .
3. Next winter I'm going to learn . . .
4. Every day Carol practices . . .
5. My parents have decided . . .
6. I've considered . . .
7. Are you thinking about . . .
8. I'm going to quit . . .
9. Why do I keep on . . .
10. My doctor says I should stop . . .
11. Jane really likes to . . .
12. Albert can't stand . . .
13. Are you going to continue to . . .
14. Walter doesn't want to start . . .
15. Next semester Gloria is going to begin . . .
16. You can't keep on . . .

Page 72 F. PROBLEMS

1. eating
   to eat/eating
2. to speak/speaking
3. practicing/playing
   to practice/to play/practicing/playing
4. to play/playing
   playing
5. working
   working
   to get/getting

1.	b	9.	a
2.	a	10.	b
3.	a	11.	a
4.	b	12.	a
5.	a	13.	b
6.	a	14.	a
7.	b	15.	a
8.	b	16.	b

1.	b	7.	c
2.	c	8.	a
3.	b	9.	b
4.	a	10.	a
5.	a	11.	c
6.	b	12.	b

GRAMMAR

Past Perfect Tense

I He She It We You They	had eaten.

I He She It We You They	hadn't eaten.

Past Perfect Continuous Tense

I He She It We You They	had been eating.

FUNCTIONS

Asking for and Reporting Information

I heard that *Arnold failed his driver's test.*

Have you heard about *Harry?*

What happened?
What went wrong?

He *broke* his *leg.*
She *sprained* her *wrist.*

How did *he* do that?

He was *playing soccer*... and he had never *played soccer* before.

I hadn't *swum in the ocean* in a long time.

Did *Mr. and Mrs. Jones drive to the beach last weekend?*
No. *They* had just *driven to the beach the weekend before.*

Did you *get to the plane* on time?
No, I didn't. By the time *I got to the plane, it* had already *taken off.*

What were you preparing for?
What had you done?
What had you forgotten to do?
What had you planned to do?
What had you done beforehand?
How long had you been planning to do it?
How long had you been preparing for that?
What did you accomplish?

Is it true?
Yes, it is.

Responding to Information

That's terrible!

Sympathizing

Poor *Harry!*

Expressing Regret

It's really a shame.

Expressing Hope

I hope *he feels better soon.*

Inquiring about Feelings-Emotions

Were you upset?
Were you disappointed?

Describing Feelings-Emotions

I feel nostalgic when _____.
I felt foolish when _____.
I was furious when _____.
I was heartbroken when _____.

Inquiring about Satisfaction

Did you enjoy *swimming last weekend?*

Expressing Want-Desire

They didn't want to.

NEW VOCABULARY

accomplish	dinner table	health foods	merry-go-round	shovel (v)
ahead of time	discuss	heart attack	nostalgic	steak bone
ankle	do poorly	heartbroken	opera	sprain (v)
balcony	doorbell	"hide and seek"	outskirts	take a course
beforehand	driver's manual	home town	oven	tango
bone	driveway	homemade	parade	travelers checks
break up	driving school	ice cream shop	pass a test	true
bring along	earn	imported (adj)	pass by	twist (v)
bump into	eat out	in advance	perfectly	visit (n)
cancel	end (n)	in case	plan (v)	voice
canoeing	experience (n)	injure	plane ticket	water (v)
catch a cold	extra	invitation	popcorn	window shopping
ceremony	fail	kid	promotion	wrestle
chess match	field	kite	purchase (v)	wrist
chew	foolish	lake	rehearse	
childhood	former	lap	remember	days gone by
choir	front teeth	look through	rent (v)	"from beginning to end
costume	get ready (for)	lose *her* voice	resume (n)	get cold feet"
course	get to	love letter	rules	it's really a shame
curtain	give a party	meeting (n)	sail away	"Poor *Harry*!
deserve	go by	memories	science	rules of the road"
dinner party	go together	memorize	science teacher	

LANGUAGE NOTES

1. **The Past Perfect Tense**

    a. The past perfect tense is formed with *had* plus the past participle of the verb.

    > *I had eaten.*
    > *They had driven.*
    > *Patty had planned to have a party.*

    b. The past perfect tense is used to refer to actions or events that occurred before a particular point in the past time.

    > *By the time I got to the plane, it **had** already **taken off**.*
    >
    > *Did Mr. and Mrs. Jones drive to the beach last weekend?*
    > *No. They **had** just **driven** to the beach the weekend before.*
    >
    > *Did George enjoy seeing his old friends last night?*
    > *Yes, he did. He **hadn't seen** his old friends in a long time.*

2. **The Past Perfect Continuous Tense**

    a. The past perfect continuous tense is formed with *had been* plus the present participle (-ing form) of the verb.

    > *I had been eating.*
    > *He had been studying.*

    b. Like the past perfect tense, the past perfect continuous tense is used to refer to events or actions that occurred before a particular point in past time. Like other continuous tenses, the past perfect continuous tense expresses the duration or ongoing character of an activity.

    > *Arnold failed his driver's test last week.*
    > *It's really a shame.*
    > *He **had been practicing** for a long time.*

3. **Irregular Past Participles**

    As in previous chapters, whenever students are required to use a new past participle that differs from the past tense form, the verb is given at the bottom of the page.

Text Pages 88–89: *They Didn't Want to*

FOCUS

> Introduction of the past perfect tense

INTRODUCING THE MODEL

1. Have students look at the model illustration.
2. Set the scene:

   a. Write the time line on the board:

   b. "Two people are talking about Mr. and Mrs. Jones. One of them wants to know what they did last weekend."

3. Present the model. Point to the appropriate time expression on the board as you present each line of the model.
4. Full-Class Choral Repetition.
5. Ask students if they have any questions; check understanding of new vocabulary: *the weekend before.*
6. Group Choral Repetition.
7. Choral Conversation.
8. Call on one or two pairs of students to present the dialog.

   (For additional practice, do Choral Conversation in small groups or by rows.)

9. Practice other verbs in the past perfect tense.

   a. Practice the verbs below whose past participles are the same as the past tense forms.

      1. Write on the board:

      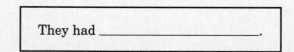

      2. Say the simple form of each verb; have students make a sentence with that verb in the past perfect tense, using the model on the board. For example:

         You: walk to school
         Student: They had walked to school.

listen to music	watch TV
talk about politics	review their lessons
work late	have a party
buy a car	wait for the bus
read the newspaper	visit some friends

b. Practice the verbs below whose past participles differ from the past tense forms.

    1. Write on the board:

```
She had _____.
```

    2. Have students make sentences as above.

eat dinner	do well on the test
take the bus	fly to London
go to school	write a letter
give John a present	drive to the airport
wear a heavy coat	get sick

SIDE BY SIDE EXERCISES

Examples

```
1.  A.  Did Mr. and Mrs. Henderson see a movie last Saturday night?
    B.  No. They didn't want to. They had just seen a movie the night before.

2.  A.  Did George eat at a restaurant yesterday evening?
    B.  No. He didn't want to. He had just eaten at a restaurant the evening before.
```

1. **Exercise 1:** Call on two students to present the dialog. Then do Choral Repetition and Choral Conversation Practice.

2. **Exercise 2:** Introduce the new expression *eat out*. Same as above.

3. **Exercises 3–13:**

```
New vocabulary:    3.  kite    4.  canoeing    7.  take a course
    9.  discuss, dinner table    10.  window-shopping
```

    Language Note

        Exercise 10:   Go window-shopping is an idiomatic expression that means *just looking around stores, store windows, and displays,* or *shopping without buying anything.*

    Either Full-Class Practice or Pair Practice.

4. **Exercise 14:** Have students use the model as a guide to create their own conversations, using vocabulary of their choice. Encourage students to use dictionaries to find new words they want to use. This exercise can be done orally in class or for written homework. If you assign it for homework, you should do one example in class to make sure students understand what's expected. Have students present their conversations in class the next day.

WORKBOOK

Page 76

EXPANSION ACTIVITY

Practice the Past Perfect Tense: Where's Martha?

1. Write on the board or on a handout for students:

Martha

Morning

get up
wash her hair
meet Jim for breakfast
borrow some books from the library
take a math test

Afternoon

eat lunch with her sister
walk to the post office to get her mail
go to history class
talk to her English teacher about her exam
do her laundry at the laundromat
buy some things

A. Have you seen Martha today?
B. Yes. I saw her this { morning / afternoon }.
    She had just _____, and she was getting ready to _____.

---

2. Set the scene: "Martha and Sally are college students. They're roommates in a dormitory at the college. It's evening now. Sally is in her room, and she's worried because Martha isn't there. She's asking other people in the dormitory if they have seen Martha." For example, she asked Bill:

    "Have you seen Martha today?"

    And Bill said:

    "Yes. I saw her this afternoon. She had just eaten lunch with her sister, and she was getting ready to walk to the post office to get her mail."

3. Role play the conversation with a few of your students; then call on pairs of students to role play. (Speaker B decides which cue to use in the answer.)

READING: *The Most Important Thing*

FOCUS

Past perfect tense

NEW VOCABULARY

ahead of time	from beginning to end	oven
bring along	heartbroken	perfectly
costume	imported (adj)	plane ticket
curtain	in advance	purchase (v)
dinner party	in case	rehearse
doorbell	invitation	resume (n)
driveway	look through	shovel
end (n)	memorize	travelers checks
foolish		water (v)

PREVIEWING THE STORY (optional)

Have students talk about the story title and/or illustrations. Introduce new vocabulary.

READING THE STORY

1. Have students read silently, or follow along silently as the story is read aloud by you, by one or more students, or on the tape.
2. Ask students if they have any questions; check understanding of vocabulary.
3. Check students' comprehension, using some or all of the following questions:

   a. What had Roger done to prepare for his dinner party?
   b. What had he forgotten to do?
   c. Why did Roger feel foolish?

   d. What had Mr. and Mrs. Jenkins done to prepare for their vacation?
   e. What had they forgotten to do?
   f. Why were they heartbroken?

   g. What had Harold done to prepare for his job interview?
   h. What had he forgotten?
   i. Why was Harold furious with himself?

   j. What had Janet done to prepare for the play?
   k. What had she forgotten to do?
   l. Why was she embarrassed?

CHECK-UP

True, False, or Maybe?

1. True	5. True
2. Maybe	6. Maybe
3. False	7. False
4. True	8. True

Choose

1. travelers checks
2. an invitation
3. borrowed
4. heartbroken
5. important
   imported

HOW ABOUT YOU?

Have students answer the questions in pairs or as a class.

Text Page 92: *They Didn't Get There on Time*

FOCUS

> The past perfect tense with *by the time* and *already*

INTRODUCING THE MODEL

1. Have students look at the model illustration.
2. Set the scene:

   a. Write on the board:

   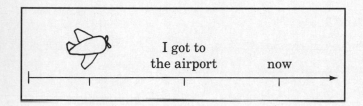

   b. "Two people are talking. One of them just missed her plane."

3. Present the model. Point to the appropriate cues on the time line on the board.
4. Full-Class Choral Repetition.
5. Ask students if they have any questions; check understanding of new vocabulary: *get to, by the time, taken off*.
6. Group Choral Repetition.
7. Choral Conversation.
8. Call on one or two pairs of students to present the dialog.

   (For additional practice, do Choral Conversation in small groups or by rows.)

SIDE BY SIDE EXERCISES

Examples

> 1. A. Did you get to the concert on time?
>   B. No, I didn't. By the time I got to the concert, it had already begun.
>
> 2. A. Did you get to the post office on time?
>   B. No, I didn't. By the time I got to the post office, it had already closed.

1. **Exercise 1:** Introduce the past participle of the verb *begin: begin–began–**begun**.* Call on two students to present the dialog. Then do Choral Repetition and Choral Conversation Practice.
2. **Exercise 2:** Introduce the past participle of the verb *close: close–closed–**closed**.* Same as above.

3. **Exercises 3–9:**

> **New vocabulary and past participles:**   3. *left*   4. *ended*   5. *started*
> 6. *meeting* (n), *finished*   8. *sail (sailed) away*   9. *parade, go (gone) by*

Either Full-Class Practice or Pair Practice.

WORKBOOK

Page 77

EXPANSION ACTIVITIES

1. *Vocabulary Review and the Past Perfect Tense*

   a. Write the following conversational model on the board:

   > A. Did you _____?
   > B. Well, . . . there was a problem: _____.
   >   By the time I got to the _____ had _____.
   > A. That's too bad.

   b. Write the following on cue cards:

get my medicine	talk to the mechanic about our car
mail my letter	enjoy the Beethoven symphony
buy the milk and orange juice we needed	wish your parents "Bon Voyage" before
cash the check	their cruise to the Bahamas
have a good flight	enjoy the first act of "Hamlet"
enjoy Professor Taylor's slides of ancient Greece	

   c. Have pairs of students create conversations based on the model on the board. Give the cue card to one member of the pair. The other person has to tell about a problem he or she had, based on Speaker A's question. Model the following example for the class:

   > A. Did you get my medicine?
   > B. Well, . . . there was a problem. I got stuck in traffic on Main Street.
   >   By the time I got to the drug store, it had already closed.
   > A. That's too bad.

2. *The Past Perfect Tense: No Wonder*

   a. Write on the board:

   > A. I saw _____ at _____ yesterday, and $\begin{Bmatrix} \text{he} \\ \text{she} \\ \text{they} \end{Bmatrix}$ looked very $\begin{Bmatrix} \text{upset} \\ \text{sad} \\ \text{excited} \\ \text{happy} \end{Bmatrix}$.

B. I know. $\begin{Bmatrix} \text{He} \\ \text{She} \\ \text{They} \end{Bmatrix}$ had just _____.

A. No wonder $\begin{Bmatrix} \text{he} \\ \text{she} \\ \text{they} \end{Bmatrix}$ looked so _____!

b. Divide the class into pairs. Have students create conversations based on the model and then present them to the class. For example:

A. I saw your uncle at the supermarket yesterday, and he looked very upset.
B. I know. He had just lost his wallet.
A. No wonder he looked so upset!

A. I saw Gloria at the bank yesterday, and she looked very excited!
B. I know. She had just gotten a raise.
A. No wonder she looked so excited!

Text Page 93: *He Hadn't Seen His Old Friends in a Long Time*

FOCUS

> Negative past perfect tense

INTRODUCING THE MODEL

1. Have students look at the model illustration.
2. Set the scene: "Two people are talking about George. George went to a party last night and saw a lot of his old friends."
3. Present the model.
4. Full-Class Choral Repetition.
5. Ask students if they have any questions; check understanding of vocabulary.
6. Group Choral Repetition.
7. Choral Conversation.
8. Call on one or two pairs of students to present the dialog.

    (For additional practice, do Choral Conversation in small groups or by rows.)
9. Expand the model with further substitution practice. Substitute *you* and names of students in your class in place of *George*. For example:

    A. Did you enjoy seeing your old friends last night?
    B. Yes, I did. I hadn't seen my old friends in a long time.

    A. Did (Mary and Jim) enjoy seeing their old friends last night?
    B. Yes, they did. They hadn't seen their old friends in a long time.

SIDE BY SIDE EXERCISES

Examples

> 1. A. Did you enjoy swimming in the ocean last weekend?
>   B. Yes, I did. I hadn't swum in the ocean in a long time.
>
> 2. A. Did Janice enjoy singing with the choir last Sunday?
>   B. Yes, she did. She hadn't sung with the choir in a long time.

1. **Exercise 1:** Review the past participle of the verb *swim: swim–swam–swum*. Call on two students to present the dialog. Then do Choral Repetition and Choral Conversation Practice.
2. **Exercise 2:** Introduce the past participle of *sing: sing–sang–sung*. Introduce the new word *choir*. Same as above.
3. **Exercises 3–9:**

> **New vocabulary and review of past participles:**   3. *taken*
>   4. *going (gone) out for dinner*   5. *visited*   6. *had*
>   7. *former, seen*   8. *played, "hide and seek"*   9. *read, love letter*

Culture Note

Exercise 8: *Hide and Seek* is a favorite game of young children in which one person *hides* and the others *seek* (look for) the person who is hiding.

Either Full-Class Practice or Pair Practice.

WORKBOOK

Page 78

Exercise Note

Workbook p. 78: In sentences 4–8, students use any vocabulary they wish. Have students compare their answers.

EXPANSION ACTIVITIES

1. *Verb Review*

   a. Write the following on the board:

drive	fly	ride	sing
eat	give	run	speak

   That's because _____ hadn't _____ $\begin{cases} \text{in a long time.} \\ \text{before.} \end{cases}$

   b. Say the sentences below and have students respond, using an appropriate verb and the sentence pattern on the board. For example:

   Teacher: Tom had too much pizza last night.
   Student: That's because he hadn't eaten pizza in a long time.

   Sentences:

   1. Tom had too much pizza last night.
   2. Mrs. Perry's daughter was very nervous before their flight to California yesterday.
   3. Mr. Walters was afraid to take his car into New York City last weekend.
   4. Mrs. Jones was very nervous before the marathon race last Sunday.
   5. Tim Flynn, the movie actor, wasn't looking forward to making a western movie last year.
   6. Carmen was feeling nervous before choir practice last week.
   7. The President practiced his Spanish all weekend before the ambassador from Venezuela arrived.
   8. Martin turned green yesterday when the nurse at the Blood Bank started taking his blood.

2. *Have You Seen _____?*

   a. Write on the board:

   A. Have you seen _____ since $\begin{cases} \text{he} \\ \text{she} \\ \text{they} \end{cases}$ _____?

   B. No, I haven't. The last time I saw _____, _____ hadn't _____ yet.

b. Write these cues on word cards:

1. (Kathy)/have her baby
2. (Joe)/move to his new apartment
3. (Alice)/go to Tokyo
4. (George)/take his English exam
5. (Barbara)/win the lottery
6. (Ted)/begin studying French
7. (Julie)/run in the marathon
8. (Tom)/meet his new girlfriend
9. (Sally)/speak to her boss
10. (Alan)/grow a beard
11. (Shirley)/finish high school
12. (Mr. and Mrs. Simon)/buy a new car
13. (Bob and Mary)/get married
14. (Mr. Jones)/have the operation
15. (Mrs. Peters)/find a job
16. (Nancy)/quit her job
17. (Ted)/stop smoking
18. (Betsy)/decide to move to Europe
19. (Sam)/learn to swim
20. (Mr. Thompson)/lose weight

c. Have pairs of students role play the conversation. Give each pair a word card as a cue for the conversation. Examples:

1. A. Have you seen Kathy since she had her baby?
   B. No, I haven't. The last time I saw her she hadn't had her baby yet.

2. A. Have you seen Joe since he moved to his new apartment?
   B. No, I haven't. The last time I saw him, he hadn't moved to his new apartment yet.

d. Have students use the model to make up new conversations, using any vocabulary they wish.

READING: *Days Gone By*

FOCUS

```
Past perfect tense
```

NEW VOCABULARY

balcony	home town	nostalgic
bump into	ice cream shop	outskirts
childhood	kid	pass by
days gone by	lake	popcorn
experience	memories	remember
field	merry-go-round	science teacher
homemade		visit (n)

PREVIEWING THE STORY (optional)

Have students talk about the story title and/or illustrations. Introduce new vocabulary.

READING THE STORY

1. Have students read silently, or follow along silently as the story is read aloud by you, by one or more students, or on the tape.

2. Ask students if they have any questions; check understanding of vocabulary.

3. Check students' comprehension, using some or all of the following questions:

   a. What did Michael do last month?
   b. Why was Michael's visit to Fullerton very special to him?
   c. Where did he walk, and what did he remember?
   d. What did he pass by?
   e. Where did he stand for a while, and what did he think about?
   f. What did he have at the ice cream shop?
   g. What did he do in the park?
   h. Where did he go fishing?
   i. Why did Michael feel like a kid again?
   j. Who did Michael visit?
   k. Who did he say hello to?
   l. Who did he bump into?
   m. What did Michael remember during his visit to his home town?
   n. Why was his trip back to Fullerton a very nostalgic experience for him?

CHECK-UP

True, False, or Maybe?

1. False	5. Maybe
2. True	6. True
3. False	7. True
4. True	8. Maybe

Choose

1. park
2. before
3. movies
4. start
5. invitation
6. realize

Listening

Have students complete the exercises as you play the tape or read the following:

Listen and choose the best answer.

1. I hadn't seen that movie before. (a)
2. I haven't gone swimming in years. (b)
3. Has the play started yet? (b)
4. Michael, please go upstairs and do your homework! (b)
5. Why did Carmen do well on the History test? (a)
6. I enjoyed dinner at Stanley's Restaurant last night. (a)

HOW ABOUT YOU?

Have students answer the questions in pairs or as a class.

Text Pages 96–97: *Have You Heard About Harry?*

FOCUS

> Contrast of the past perfect and past continuous tenses

INTRODUCING THE MODEL

1. Have students look at the model illustration.
2. Set the scene: "Harry had an accident recently. Two of his friends are talking about him."
3. Present the model.
4. Full-Class Choral Repetition.
5. Ask students if they have any questions; check understanding of vocabulary.
6. Group Choral Repetition.
7. Choral Conversation.
8. Call on one or two pairs of students to present the dialog.

   (For additional practice, do Choral Conversation in small groups or by rows.)

SIDE BY SIDE EXERCISES

Examples

---

1. A. Have you heard about Tom?
   B. No, I haven't. What happened?
   A. He twisted his ankle last week.
   B. That's terrible! How did he do that?
   A. He was flying a kite . . . and he had never flown a kite before.
   B. Poor Tom! I hope he feels better soon.

2. A. Have you heard about Doris?
   B. No, I haven't. What happened?
   A. She sprained her wrist last week.
   B. That's terrible! How did she do that?
   A. She was playing tennis . . . and she had never played tennis before.
   B. Poor Doris! I hope she feels better soon.

---

1. **Exercise 1:** Introduce the new words *twist, ankle.* Call on two students to present the dialog. Then do Choral Repetition and Choral Conversation Practice.

2. **Exercise 2:** Introduce the new words *sprain, wrist.* Same as above.

3. **Exercises 3–9:**

   > **New vocabulary:**   6. *injure, wrestle*   7. *front teeth, chew, steak bone*
   > 8. *lose her voice, opera*   9. *tango*

4. **Exercise 10:** Have students use the model as a guide to create their own conversations, using vocabulary of their choice. Encourage students to use dictionaries to find new words they want to use. This exercise can be done orally in class or for written homework. If you assign it for homework, you should do one example in class to make sure students understand what's expected. Have students present their conversations in class the next day.

Pages 79–80 (Exercise D)

EXPANSION ACTIVITIES

1. Past Perfect Tense: Finish the Sentence

a. Write on the board:

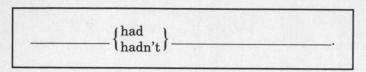

b. Read the cues below and call on several students to finish each sentence, using verbs in the past perfect tense:

1. (Martha) was very tired yesterday morning because . . .
2. (Joe) was very hungry at dinner last night because . . .
3. (Mr. Jones) didn't have any clean clothes to wear last weekend because . . .
4. (Robert) didn't do very well on his English test yesterday because . . .
5. (Charles) didn't get to the airport on time yesterday because . . .
6. (Peggy) didn't get the job as a secretary last week because . . .
7. (Irene) was very nervous during the interview yesterday because . . .
8. (Brian) was really excited about visiting Mexico last summer because . . .
9. (Barbara) was very well prepared for her exam last Friday because . . .
10. (Mr. and Mrs. Green) didn't go to a movie last night because . . .

Example:

You:	Martha was very tired yesterday morning because . . .
Students:	she had studied for an English test until 2 A.M.
	she hadn't slept well.
	she had had terrible nightmares all night.
	her neighbor's dog had barked until after midnight.

2. How Did It Happen?

Text pages 96 and 97 deal with accidents or unfortunate things that happened to various people. Have students tell about similar experiences they might have had. Possible questions are:

a. Have you ever broken your leg or arm? How did it happen?
b. Have you ever twisted your ankle? How did it happen?
c. Have you ever sprained your wrist or your back? How did it happen?
d. Have you ever gotten into an accident? What happened?
e. Have you ever lost your voice? Tell about it.

This activity may be done as a class discussion or in pairs, where students ask each other the questions and then report back to the class about the other person.

Variation:

For homework, have students write about an accident or unfortunate experience they have had. Collect the papers and distribute them randomly to students in the class. Have those students read the papers to the class and have others try to guess who this unfortunate event happened to.

Text Pages 98–99: *It's Really a Shame*

FOCUS

Introduction of the past perfect continuous tense

GETTING READY

Introduce the past perfect continuous tense.

1. Write on the board:

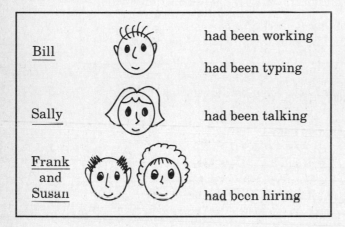

Bill		had been working
		had been typing
Sally		had been talking
Frank and Susan		had been hiring

2. Point to the appropriate cues on the board as you tell the following story:

   "I went to see some of my old friends at the PRESTO Company yesterday afternoon. Everybody was happy to see me, but they were all EXHAUSTED."

   a. They *had been working* very hard all day.
   b. Bill *had been typing* all day.
   c. Sally *had been talking* on the telephone all day.
   d. And Frank and Susan *had been hiring* new employees all day.

3. Have students repeat sentences 1–4 chorally and individually.

4. Form sentences with the words in the box at the top of text page 98. Have students repeat chorally. For example:

   "I had been eating."
   "He had been eating."

INTRODUCING THE MODEL

1. Have students look at the model illustration.
2. Set the scene: "Arnold took his driver's test last week, but he didn't do very well. Two of his friends are talking about what happened."
3. Present the model.
4. Full-Class Choral Repetition.

5. Ask students if they have any questions; check understanding of new vocabulary: *fail, true.*
6. Group Choral Repetition.
7. Choral Conversation.
8. Call on one or two pairs of students to present the dialog.

(For additional practice, do Choral Conversation in small groups or by rows.)

SIDE BY SIDE EXERCISES

Examples

1. A. I heard that Lucy lost her job at the bank last week. Is it true?
   B. Yes, it is . . . and it's really a shame. She had been working there for a long time.
2. A. I heard that Boris lost the chess match last week. Is it true?
   B. Yes, it is . . . and it's really a shame. He had been practicing for a long time.

1. **Exercise 1:** Call on two students to present the dialog. Then do Choral Repetition and Choral Conversation Practice.

2. **Exercise 2:** Introduce the new word *match*. Same as above.

3. **Exercises 3–10:**

New vocabulary: 3. *break up, go together*   4. *do poorly*   5. *cancel, plan* (v)
7. *heart attack*   10. *catch a cold*

Culture Note

Exercise 3: The expressions *go together* and *break up* are associated with dating customs in the United States. When two teenagers date each other exclusively, we say they are *going together.* When this type of relationship ends, we say they have *broken up.*

Either Full-Class Practice or Pair Practice.

WORKBOOK

Pages 80–81 (Exercises E, F)

EXPANSION ACTIVITIES

1. *Practice the Past Continuous Tense*

   a. Write on the board:

   Yes. _____ had been _____ing for _____.

b. Ask students the questions below. Have students answer individually, using any time expression they wish after *for*. For example:

>You: Was it snowing when you got up this morning?
>Student: Yes. It had been snowing for several hours.

1. Were the musicians playing when you arrived at the concert?
2. Had (Bill) started smoking yet when you met him?
3. Was Professor Jones already teaching when you came to class?
4. Had (Bob) started driving trucks for a living when you met him?
5. Had (Mary) started to study Algebra when she went to college?
6. Had (Mr. and Mrs. Smith) already started to paint their house when you saw them last week?
7. Did Maria speak English when she moved to the United States?
8. Was it raining when you went to bed last night?
9. Did you play baseball before you went to high school?
10. Were your friends eating when you got to the restaurant last night?
11. Had (Richard) already started looking for a job when you saw him last week?
12. Were people dancing when you got to the party?

2. *When Your Parents Were Young*

a. Write on the board:

>A. Did _____ when your parents were young?
>B. Yes. _____ had been _____ing for _____.
>   or
>No. _____ hadn't started _____ yet.

b. Use cues such as those below to create conversations about how things have changed since your students' parents were young. Write some or all of these cues on the board. Have students think of others.

people
- wear jeans
- watch TV
- drive cars
- travel by airplane
- listen to jazz
- listen to rock music
- eat frozen food
- eat a lot of junk food

men
- wear their hair long
- grow beards

women
- have jobs
- wear pants
- wear their hair short

c. Call on pairs of students to create conversations. For example:

>A. Did people wear jeans when your parents were young?
>B. Yes. They had been wearing jeans for several years.
>   or
>No. They hadn't started wearing jeans yet.

3. Role Play: Good News/Bad News

a. Write the following conversational model on the board:

A. Hi, _____. What's new?

B. _____.

A. That's great! Congratulations!

_____ had been _____ing _____.

   or

That's a shame! I'm sorry to hear that.

_____ had been _____ing _____.

---

b. Have pairs of students create conversations based on the conversational model. Give one member of the pair a situation card as a cue for the role play. The other student must react appropriately to either the good news or the bad news. Possible situations are:

> You finally passed your driver's test.
> Your wife/husband just lost his/her job.
> Your wife/husband just got promoted.
> You just broke up with your boyfriend/girlfriend.
> You just got engaged.
> You did very badly on your (English) exam.
> You did very well on your (English) exam.
> You hurt your back and couldn't be in the school play last weekend.
> You had to cancel your trip to Mexico because you sprained your ankle.

Examples:

> A. Hi, Joe. What's new?
> B. I finally passed my driver's test.
> A. That's great! Congratulations! You had been preparing for it for a long time.

> A. Hi, Barbara. What's new?
> B. My husband just lost his job at Green's Supermarket.
> A. That's a shame! I'm sorry to hear that. He had been working there for many years.

Text Page 100

READING: *Nobody Was Surprised*

FOCUS

> Past perfect continuous tense

NEW VOCABULARY

accomplish	driving school	health foods
deserve	earn	pass a test
driver's manual	extra	"rules of the road"

PREVIEWING THE STORY (optional)

Have students talk about the story title and/or illustrations. Introduce new vocabulary.

READING THE STORY

1. Have students read silently, or follow along silently as the story is read aloud by you, by one or more students, or on the tape.
2. Ask students if they have any questions; check understanding of vocabulary.
3. Check students' comprehension, using some or all of the following questions:

    a. What did Stella Karp win last week?
    b. What had she been doing every morning?
    c. What had she been doing for several months?
    d. What had she been doing every day after work?
    e. Why did she deserve to win the marathon?

    f. What did my friend Stuart pass the other day?
    g. What had he been doing for several months?
    h. What had he been doing for the past several weeks?
    i. What had he been studying since he was a little boy?
    j. Why did he deserve to pass his driver's test?

    k. What did Sally Compton get last week?
    l. What had she been doing for several months?
    m. What had she been studying in the evening?
    n. What had she been doing on the weekends?
    o. Why did she deserve to get a promotion?

IN YOUR OWN WORDS

1. Make sure students understand the instructions.
2. Have students do the activity as written homework, using a dictionary for any new words they wish to use.
3. Have students present and discuss what they have written, in pairs or as a class.

ON YOUR OWN: *Plans That "Fell Through"*

FOCUS

Review of the past perfect and past perfect continuous tenses

ON YOUR OWN ACTIVITY

There are three situations on this page. Introduce and practice each separately. For each situation:

1. Have students cover the text of the story with a piece of paper and look at the illustration to the left.

2. Read the situation one or two times. See how much students have understood by asking a few questions. For example:

> Situation 1:   What had Patty planned to do last weekend?
> What had she done before the party?
> Why did she have to cancel the party?

> Situation 2:   What had Michael planned to do last week?
> How had he been preparing to ask for a raise?
> Did he get the raise? Why not?

> Situation 3:   What had John and Julia planned to do last month?
> What had they done before the wedding?
> Did they get married? Why not?

3. Have students uncover the text and follow along as you read the situation again. Check understanding of new vocabulary.

New vocabulary: 1. *get ready (for)*   3. *ceremony, rent* (v), *"get cold feet"*

Language Note

Situation 3: *Get cold feet* is most often used when someone fails to carry out or follow through with an important plan, such as a wedding or wedding proposal, asking someone out on a date, or applying for an important job.

4. Have students tell about plans they had that *fell through,* using the questions at the bottom of the page as a guide. Introduce the new word *beforehand.* This can be done orally as Full-Class Practice or Pair Practice, or for written homework.

WORKBOOK

Pages 81–83 (Exercises G, H, I)
Check-Up Test: Pages 84–85

WORKBOOK ANSWER KEY AND LISTENING SCRIPTS

Page 76 A. BEFORE

1. had, visited
2. had, gotten
3. had done
4. had, baked
5. had given
6. had, bought
7. had gone
8. had, driven
9. had, hurt
10. had spent
11. had, left
12. had lost
13. had grown
14. had eaten

Page 77 B. LATE FOR EVERYTHING

1. had, begun
2. had, gone
3. had, given
4. had, left
5. had, started
6. had, closed
7. had arrived
8. had gotten

Page 78 C. TOM TOUGH

1. He visited his friends, He hadn't visited them
2. He drove his motorcycle, He hadn't driven his motorcycle
3. He went bowling, He hadn't gone bowling
4. . . . .
5. . . . .
6. . . . .
7. . . . .

Page 79 D. WORKING HARD

1. She was studying for her math examination.
2. She had already written an English composition.
3. She hadn't reviewed her French lessons yet.
4. She hadn't read the next history lesson yet.

5. They were lifting weights.
6. They had already gone jogging.
7. They had already swum across the pool 100 times.
8. They hadn't taken a karate lesson yet.

9. He was building a birdhouse for his cousins.
10. He had already drawn a picture for his mother.
11. He hadn't written a story for his father yet.
12. He hadn't knitted a sweater for Rover yet.

Page 80 E. WHAT HAD THEY BEEN DOING?

1. had been living
2. had been practicing
3. had been writing
4. had been working
5. had been planning

Page 81 F. WHAT ARE THEY SAYING?

1. had been looking
2. had been studying
3. had been working
4. had been going
5. had been looking forward to
6. had been drinking
7. had been planning

H. MA__Y __OU'S B__OKEN
           TYPEW__ITE__

1.

Robert,
   I'm afraid there's
something wrong with the
radiator in the living
room. Also, the
refrigerator is broken.
I called the landlord
and complained. He'll
try to repair both the
radiator and the
refrigerator tomorrow.
         Mary Lou

2.

Louise,
   I'm terribly worried about my
brother Larry's health. He
hasn't been feeling very well
recently. According to Doctor
Larson, Larry is having
problems with his blood
pressure. He really should
try to relax and take life a
little easier.
         Mary Lou

3.

Roger,
   Here's how to get to Irene's house. Drive along Central
Street until you reach the Greenville library. Turn
right. Drive a little longer (one more mile) and turn
left at the corner of River and Green Streets. Irene lives
in the dark brown apartment building across from the
laundromat and the playground. Her address is Fourteen
River Street. I'm sure you'll find her apartment easily.
         Mary Lou

4.

Rosa,
   I'll be flying to Rome
on Friday, and I'll be
returning three days later.
Can you please drive me to the
airport? The plane leaves
on Friday morning at eleven
o'clock.
       All my love,
       Mary Lou

5.

Arnold,
   Can you recommend a
restaurant in your
neighborhood? I'm planning
to take my relatives to lunch
tomorrow, but I'm not sure
where. We've already tried
the English Tea Room, but we
didn't like their fruit
salad. You and Gregory had
lunch at an excellent
restaurant last week. Do
you remember the name of the
place?
       Your friend,
       Mary Lou

Page 83 I. LISTEN

Listen to each sentence. Put a circle around the
appropriate answer.

Ex. Doris lost her voice.

1. My ankle hurts a lot.
2. I just canceled my trip.
3. Roger has failed all his tests this year.
4. We flew our kites all day yesterday.
5. Have you heard that Margaret sprained her wrist?
6. Is Alice one of your relatives?
7. I went window-shopping during my lunch hour this afternoon.
8. I feel terrible. Lisa and I have just broken up.
9. Grandfather can't chew this piece of steak very well.
10. Do you think Sally will take a day off soon?
11. What did you and your students discuss in class?
12. Did you see the parade go by?
13. Michael has been writing invitations all day.
14. I have an important decision to make.
15. Patty was going to ask for a raise, but she got cold feet.
16. I envy you.

Answers

1. b	9. a
2. c	10. a
3. b	11. b
4. c	12. c
5. b	13. a
6. c	14. c
7. a	15. c
8. c	16. b

CHECK-UP TEST: *CHAPTERS 7–8*

Page 84   A.

1. eating
2. smoking
3. to move
4. swimming
5. Dancing
6. to play
7. talking
8. getting up

Page 84   B.

1. hadn't spoken
2. had, done
3. had, left
4. hadn't written

5. had given
6. hadn't worn
7. hadn't eaten

Page 85   C.

1. had been practicing
2. had been planning
3. had been looking forward
4. had been arguing

Page 85   D.

Listen and put a circle around the correct answer.

Ex. Janet likes to . . .

1. You really should quit . . . .
2. I'm thinking about . . . .
3. My parents are considering . . . .
4. Harry is going to start to . . . .
5. Sara enjoys . . . .
6. I think Professor Thompson should continue . . . .

Answers

1. a
2. b
3. b
4. b
5. b
6. b

GRAMMAR

Two-Word Verbs: Separable

I'm going to	put on my boots. put my boots on. put them on.

bring back the TV—bring it back	put away the clothes—put them away
call up Sally—call her up	put on your boots—put them on
clean up the living room—clean it up	take back the books—take them back
cross out the mistakes—cross them out	take down the decorations—take them down
do over the homework—do it over	take off your boots—take them off
drop off my sister—drop her off	take out the garbage—take it out
figure out the bill—figure it out	think over the decision—think it over
fill out the form—fill it out	throw away the notebook—throw it away
give back the ring—give it back	throw out the magazines—throw them out
hand in your homework—hand it in	try on the pants—try them on
hang up the portrait—hang it up	turn down the job offer—turn it down
look up the definition—look it up	turn off the oven—turn it off
pick out her gown—pick it out	turn on the heat—turn it on
pick up her clothes—pick them up	write down the number—write it down

Two-Word Verbs: Inseparable

I	hear from George hear from him <s>hear George from</s> <s>hear him from</s>	very often.

call on	look through
get along with	look up to
get over	pick on
hear from	run into
look for	take after

FUNCTIONS

Extending an Invitation

Would you like to *go fishing this morning*?
Would you like to get together *today*?

Are you free *after you take them back*?

Declining an Invitation

I'd like to, but I can't.
I'd really like to, but I can't.
I'm afraid I can't.

Expressing Inability

I can't.
I'm afraid I can't.

Expressing Obligation

I have to *fill out my income tax form*.

I've really got to do it.

Asking for and Reporting Information

What size do you wear?
Size 32, I think.

How much *does it* cost?
The *usual* price is
_____ dollars.

Inquiring about Intention

Will you *take it back*?

When are you going to *call up your cousin*?

Expressing Intention

I'm going to *call him up next week*.
I'll *call you in the morning*.
I'll *turn it off* right away.

Inquiring about Remembering

Did you remember to *turn off the oven*?

Forgetting

I completely forgot!

Asking for Advice

Do you think I should *keep these old love letters*?

Offering Advice

I think you should *throw them away*.

Offering a Suggestion

Let's *get together tomorrow instead*.

Why don't you *look through all of our raincoats and pick out the one you like*?

Offering to Help

May I help you?

Expressing Want-Desire

I'm looking for *a raincoat*.

Do you have any *raincoats* that are *a little lighter*?

NEW VOCABULARY

accept
accident report
accidentally
Algebra
answer (n)
apparently
baggy
bring back
button
call on
call up
check (v)
child rearing
Christmas decorations
clean up
cleaner's
college application
　form
Colorado
constantly
correct (adj)
cross out

decorations
definition
Denver
discouraged (adj)
do over
dressing room
drop off
erase
especially
eventually
ex-boyfriend
extra large
feel like
figure out
final
fit
free
get along with
get over
give back
go with
hand in

hang up
happiness
hear from
heat (n)
help (n)
hospital bill
incorrectly
insurance form
job offer
keep
kiss (v)
leave on
library book
look up
look up to
loose
medium
narrow
New Year
notice (v)
on sale
paper

party decorations
percent
pick on
pick out
plaid
put away
refund (n)
refuse (v)
regular
report
run into
sale
selection
simply
size
so far
take after
take back
take down
think over
throw away
throw out

tight
toy
trousers
try on
turn down
turn off
use up
usual
wedding guest
wedding invitation
within
write down
zipper

give it right back
I completely forgot
in the first place
My pleasure.
No problem at all.
Speak to you then.
That'll be great.
You're in luck!

LANGUAGE NOTES

Two-Word Verbs

A two-word verb consists of a main verb plus a *particle*. In most cases, the addition of the particle changes the meaning of the verb. For example:

> *take* vs. *take off/take out/take back/take down/take after*

In some cases, the two-word verb is interchangeable with the main verb. For example:

> *call* or *call up*
> *clean* or *clean up*

1. With separable two-word verbs,

   a. A noun object may be placed either between the parts of the verb or after the verb. For example:

   > ***fill*** *the form* ***out***
   > ***fill out*** *the form*

   b. A pronoun object may be placed *only between* the two parts of the verb. For example:

   > ***hang*** *it* ***up***
   > ***pick*** *him* ***up***
   > ***call*** *her* ***up***

2. With inseparable two-word verbs, a noun or pronoun object must always *follow* the verb. For example:

   > ***hear from*** $\begin{Bmatrix} Paul \\ him \end{Bmatrix}$
   > ***look for*** $\begin{Bmatrix} the\ book \\ it \end{Bmatrix}$

Text Page 104: *Sometime Next Week*

FOCUS

- Introduction of the following separable two-word verbs:

bring back	*hang up*	*put away*
call up	*pick up*	*throw out*
fill out	*pick out*	*turn on*

- Practice separating these verbs with pronouns

INTRODUCING THE MODEL

1. Have students look at the model illustration.
2. Set the scene: "Two friends are talking. One of them is upset because his TV is broken. A repairman is fixing it, but it isn't ready yet."
3. Present the model.
4. Full-Class Choral Repetition.
5. Ask students if they have any questions; check understanding of the two-word verb *bring back*.
6. Group Choral Repetition.
7. Choral Conversation.
8. Call on one or two pairs of students to present the dialog.

   (For additional practice, do Choral Conversation in small groups or by rows.)
9. Read the verbs in the box at the top of the page, which show how other two-word verbs can be separated by a pronoun:

"bring back the TV"	"call up Sally"	"put away the clothes"
"bring it back"	"call her up"	"put them away"

SIDE BY SIDE EXERCISES

Examples

---

1. A. When are you going to call up your cousin in Chicago?
   B. I'm going to call him up sometime next week.

2. A. When is Peter going to fill out his college application forms?
   B. He's going to fill them out sometime next week.

---

1. **Exercise 1:**

   a. Set the scene: "John has a cousin in Chicago. They call each other a lot."
   b. Introduce the new verb *call up*.
   c. Call on two students to present the dialog. Then do Choral Repetition and Choral Conversation Practice.

2. **Exercise 2:** Review the two-word verbs *fill out* and *college application form*. Call on two students to present the dialog. Then do Choral Repetition and Choral Conversation Practice.

3. **Exercises 3–9:**

New vocabulary: 3. *pick up, cleaner's*   4. *pick out, wedding gown*
   5. *put away*   6. *take back, library book*   7. *turn on, heat* (n)   8. *throw out*
   9. *hang up*

Culture Note

Exercise 5:   People living in cold climates in the United States typically store their winter clothes in an attic or chest during the summer months. This custom has two purposes: it gets the heavy clothes out of one's way, and it protects woolen clothes from being eaten by moths.

Either Full-Class Practice or Pair Practice.

As you introduce each new two-word verb, read the corresponding *set the scene* below.

3. "Greta took some clothes to the cleaner's last week. She needs to go back there this week to get them."
4. "Maria is going to get married soon. She's been shopping for a wedding dress, but she hasn't found one that she really likes. She just can't decide."
5. "Many people wear heavy clothes in the winter. During the summer they don't need these clothes so they keep them someplace else."
6. "Brian borrowed a lot of books from the library a few weeks ago, and he still has them."
7. "A woman is visiting her friends. She isn't very comfortable because there's no heat in the apartment."
8. "Margaret hates to clean her apartment. She has a lot of old magazines that she doesn't need."
9. "That portrait of you is very nice. I think you should put it on your wall."

WORKBOOK

Page 86

EXPANSION ACTIVITIES

1. ***What's the Verb?***

   a. Write on the board:

   ---

bring back	pick up
call up	put away
fill out	throw out
hang up	turn on
pick out	

   I'm going to _____ soon.

   ---

   b. Say each object cue on the next page. For each one, have students choose a two-word verb that fits the object and make a sentence using the model on the board. For example:

   You: Uncle Bill
   Student: I'm going to *call up* Uncle Bill soon.

1. the job application form (fill out)
2. some friends at the airport (pick up)
3. tickets at the symphony (pick up)
4. the garbage (take out)
5. these old shoes (throw out)
6. my summer clothes (put away)
7. the TV at the repair shop (pick up)
8. the food that I just bought (put away)
9. my new photographs (hang up)
10. a new pair of shoes for the wedding (pick out)
11. the hammer and screwdriver you borrowed (bring back)
12. the heat (turn on)
13. my income tax form (fill out)
14. those old souvenirs we don't want anymore (throw out)
15. my sister at the dentist's office (pick up)
16. Mr. and Mrs. Jones (call up)

2. *Finish the Sentence*

Begin each sentence below. Have students repeat it and an appropriate object after the verb. For example:

> Teacher: She turned on . . . .
> Student: She turned on the light.
>   or
>   She turned on the heat.

Sentences:

1. She turned on . . .
2. We called up . . .
3. He put away . . .
4. She hung up . . .
5. They brought back . . .
6. We threw out . . .
7. I picked up . . .
8. I picked out . . .
9. He filled out . . .

3. *Forming Two-Word Verbs*

a. Write on the board:

> A. Don't forget to _____.
> B. Don't worry. I won't forget to _____.

call _____	a tie
fill _____	the application
hang _____	the dishes
pick _____	the lights
put _____	your records
throw _____	the old newspapers
turn _____	your aunt
	the TV
	your clothes

b. Have students create conversations based on the model and the word cues on the board. Students must combine the verbs with appropriate particles and objects. For example:

> A. Don't forget to fill out the application.
> B. Don't worry. I won't forget to fill it out.

Text Page 105: *I Completely Forgot!*

FOCUS

- Practice separating two-word verbs with pronouns and nouns
- Introduction of the following separable two-word verbs:

hand in	*take off*	*turn off*
put on	*take out*	

INTRODUCING THE MODEL

This model should be presented twice: once with the object noun after the verb *(turn off the oven)* and once with the noun between the two parts of the verb *(turn the oven off)*.

1. Have students look at the model illustration.
2. Set the scene: "A husband and wife are having dinner together. They turned on the oven while they were cooking dinner, and it's still on."
3. Present the model.
4. Full-Class Choral Repetition.
5. Ask students if they have any questions; check understanding of new vocabulary: *turn off, I completely forgot!*
6. Group Choral Repetition.
7. Choral Conversation.
8. Call on one or two pairs of students to present the dialog.
9. Expand the model with further substitution practice. Call on pairs of students to present the model, using *the lights, the radio.*

   (For additional practice, do Choral Conversation in small groups or by rows.)

SIDE BY SIDE EXERCISES

Examples

1. A. Did you remember to take back the library books/take the library books back?
   B. Oh, no! I completely forgot! I'll take them back right away.

2. A. Did you remember to put away your toys/put your toys away?
   B. Oh, no! I completely forgot! I'll put them away right away.

1. **Exercise 1:** Call on two students to present the dialog. Then do Choral Repetition and Choral Conversation Practice.
2. **Exercise 2:** Introduce the new word *toy.* Same as above.
3. **Exercises 3–9:**

   New vocabulary: 3. *call up*   4. *accident report*   5. *hand in*   6. *take out*
   7. *take off*   8. *put on*   9. *"No Smoking" sign*

Either Full-Class Practice or Pair Practice.

As you introduce the new two-word verbs in Exercises 5–8, read the corresponding *set the scene* below.

5. "Some of the students haven't given their homework to the teacher yet."

6. "A wife is talking to her husband. She's afraid the garbage is still in the kitchen."

7. "A father is talking to his daughter. Her boots are very dirty. She shouldn't be wearing them in the house."

8. "A wife is talking to her husband. It's raining, and he isn't wearing his raincoat."

WORKBOOK

Page 87

EXPANSION ACTIVITIES

1. Warmup: Finish the Verb

Say each of the verbs below and have students add any particles they have learned to make them into two-word verbs.

Teacher	Student	Teacher	Student
bring . . .	bring back	throw . . .	throw out
call . . .	call up	turn . . .	turn on
fill . . .	fill out		turn off
hang . . .	hang up	take . . .	take out
pick . . .	pick out		take off
	pick up	hand . . .	hand in
put . . .	put away		
	put on		

2. What's the Word?

a. Write on the board:

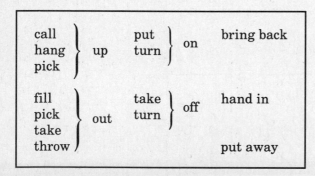

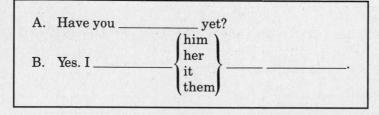

b. Point to a verb and call on a pair of students to create a conversation, using the model on the board. For example:

You: *call up*
Students: A. Have you called up Mary yet?
or
Have you called Mary up yet?
B. Yes. I called her up yesterday.

You: *hand in*
Students: A. Have you handed in your English homework yet?
or
Have you handed your English homework in yet?
B. Yes. I handed it in this morning.

3. **Listen and Pick Out the Right Answer**

a. Write the following conversational model on the board:

> A. Have you _____ yet?
> B. _____? Yes. I _____ _____ _____ a few minutes ago.

b. Have pairs of students create conversations based on the model. Give Student A a *verb cue* and Student B a card with two *object cues*. Based on the verb he or she hears, Student B must choose the correct object to complete the dialog. For example:

Student A   Student B

| turn it on | | my coat |
| | | the heat |

A. Have you turned it on yet?
B. The heat? Yes. I turned it on a few minutes ago.

Cue cards:

turn it on	my coat / the heat		hand it in	the telephone / my homework
turn it off	the stove / my jacket		put them away	my books / my children
pick it out	the accident report / a new suit		take it off	my coat / the oven
throw it out	the garbage / my new raincoat		hang them up	the portraits / the magazines

READING: *A Busy Saturday*

FOCUS

> Two-word verbs (separable)

NEW VOCABULARY

> feel like

PREVIEWING THE STORY (optional)

Have students talk about the story title and/or illustrations. Introduce new vocabulary.

READING THE STORY

1. Have students read silently, or follow along silently as the story is read aloud by you, by one or more students, or on the tape.
2. Ask students if they have any questions; check understanding of vocabulary.
3. Check students' comprehension, using some or all of the following questions:

   a. Why is everybody in the Martini family going to be very busy today?
   b. What does Mr. Martini have to do? Why?
   c. What does Mrs. Martini have to do? Why?
   d. What does Frank have to do? Why?
   e. What does Bob have to do? Why?
   f. What does Julie have to do? Why?

CHECK-UP

Q & A

1. Call on a pair of students to present the model.
2. Have students work in pairs to create new dialogs.
3. Call on pairs to present their new dialogs to the class.

HOW ABOUT YOU?

Have students do the activity in pairs or as a class.

Text Page 107: *I Don't Think So*

FOCUS

Introduction of the following separable two-word verbs:

cross out	*think over*
do over	*throw away*
give back	*turn down*
leave on	*write down*
look up	

INTRODUCING THE MODEL

1. Have students look at the model illustration.
2. Set the scene: "Two sisters are looking through some of their old things. One of them has found some old letters from a boyfriend. She doesn't really know what to do with them."
3. Present the model.
4. Full-Class Choral Repetition.
5. Ask students if they have any questions; check understanding of new vocabulary: *keep, love letters, throw away.*

   ### Language Note

   A *love letter* is an expression that refers to a letter written to one's girlfriend or boyfriend.

6. Group Choral Repetition.
7. Choral Conversation.
8. Call on one or two pairs of students to present the dialog.

   (For additional practice, do Choral Conversation in small groups or by rows.)

SIDE BY SIDE EXERCISES

Examples

---

1. A. Do you think I should keep my ex-boyfriend's ring?
   B. No. I don't think so. I think you should give it back.
2. A. Do you think I should leave the air conditioner on?
   B. No. I don't think so. I think you should turn it off.

---

1. **Exercise 1:**

   a. Set the scene: "This girl doesn't like her boyfriend anymore, but she still has his ring."
   b. Introduce the new vocabulary *keep, ex-boyfriend, give back.*
   c. Call on two students to present the dialog. Then do Choral Repetition and Choral Conversation Practice.

2. **Exercise 2:**

   a. Set the scene: "It's very hot today. Somebody turned the air conditioner on early this morning to keep the house cool. Everyone is going to go out soon."

   b. Introduce the new vocabulary *leave on*.

   c. Same as above.

3. **Exercises 3–9:**

> **New vocabulary:**   3. *do over*   4. *erase, cross out*   5. *use up, throw away*
>   6. *telephone number, write down*   7. *make my decision, think over*
>   8. *accept, job offer, turn down*   9. *definition, look up*

Language Note

   Exercise 1: *Ex-boyfriend*. The prefix *ex* means *former*. Other examples of this prefix are *ex-husband, ex-wife*.

Either Full-Class Practice or Pair Practice.

As you introduce the new two-word verb in each exercise, read the corresponding *set the scene* below.

   3. "Tom made a lot of mistakes on his homework. He's asking his mother what he should do."

   4. "Fred also made a lot of mistakes on his homework. He isn't going to do it over, but he wants to fix his mistakes."

   5. "There's a little more milk in the carton. It's old, but it's still okay to drink."

   6. "This person can't remember Sally's telephone number."

   7. "When you have a problem, it's usually a good idea to think about the problem for a while before you decide what to do."

   8. "Somebody wants to hire Mary. Should she say 'yes' or should she say 'no'?"

   9. "A lot of students use a dictionary when they don't know the definition of a word."

WORKBOOK

Page 88

EXPANSION ACTIVITIES

1. **Finish the Sentence**

   a. Write on the board:

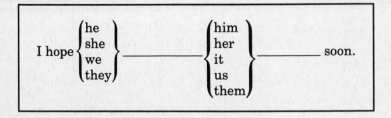

   b. Read the situations below. For each, have a student complete the statement on the board, using any correct two-word verb. For example:

You: My neighbor borrowed my radio last week.

Student: I hope she/he gives it back soon.

1. We haven't talked to David in a long time. (I hope he calls us up soon.)
2. My ex-girlfriend still has my ring. (I hope she gives it back soon.)
3. There's too much milk in the refrigerator. (I hope we use it up soon.)
4. My neighbors have a lot of garbage in front of their garage. (I hope they throw it away/throw it out soon.)
5. John has been shopping for a suit for his wedding, but he hasn't found one yet. (I hope he picks one out soon.)
6. Greta has had that college application form for weeks, and she hasn't done it yet! (I hope she fills it out soon.)
7. Bob would like to ask Louise for a date, but he's a little shy. (I hope he calls her up soon.)
8. Some of the students haven't given me their homework yet. (I hope they hand it in soon.)
9. Our neighbors are playing their record player so loudly that we can't hear each other. (I hope they turn it off soon.)
10. Aunt Helen has a job offer from the bank, but I'm sure she won't enjoy working there. (I hope she turns it down.)
11. I just arrived at the airport and I called my sister to tell her. (I hope she picks me up soon.)

2. *Choose the Right Words*

a. Write on the board:

A. Hi, _____. This is _____. Are you busy right now?

B. Not really. I was just { doing / filling / hanging / looking / putting / taking / thinking / throwing / turning / writing } _____ when you called.

b. Say each object cue below and call on a pair of students to role play this telephone conversation. Speaker B must choose the correct verb in brackets and add the correct particle. For example:

You: *the children's toys*

A. Hi, (John). This is (Robert). Are you busy right now?
B. Not really. I was just putting away the children's toys when you called.

1. some photographs (hanging up)
2. a new recipe (writing down)
3. my homework (doing over)
4. the TV (turning on/off)
5. some winter coats (putting away)
7. some tax forms (filling out)
8. the radio (turn on/off)
9. my shoes (putting on)
10. my parents' new address (writing down)
11. the lights upstairs (turning on/off)
12. some old letters (throwing out/throwing away/putting away)

3. Synonyms

a. Write on the board:

call up	give back	pick up	turn down
cross out	hand in	take back	turn off
do over	hang up	think over	use up
fill out	look up	throw away	write down

Okay. I'll _____ right away.

b. Read each of the statements below. Have students respond with an appropriate two-word verb synonym from the list on the board. For example:

Teacher: Don't forget to phone her.
Student: Okay. I'll call her up right away.

1. Don't forget to phone her. (call her up)
2. Don't forget to return this book. (take it back)
3. Please complete the form. (fill it out)
4. Don't forget to find the meaning of this word. (look it up)
5. Please get off the telephone. (hang up)
6. Please write these exercises again. (do them over)
7. Don't forget to copy Mr. Franklin's address. (write it down)
8. Don't forget to get my shirt at the cleaner's. I need it this morning. (pick it up)
9. Please fix your mistakes. (cross them out)
10. Don't forget to give the teacher your homework. (hand it in)

Text Page 108

READING: *Lucy's English Composition*

FOCUS

> Two-word verbs (separable)

NEW VOCABULARY

accidentally	correct	give it right back
apparently	Denver	incorrectly
check (v)	discouraged (adj)	in the first place
Colorado		paper

PREVIEWING THE STORY (optional)

Have students talk about the story title and/or illustration. Introduce new vocabulary.

READING THE STORY

1. Have students read silently, or follow along silently as the story is read aloud by you, by one or more students, or on the tape.
2. Ask students if they have any questions; check understanding of vocabulary.
3. Check students' comprehension, using some or all of the following questions:

   a. Why is Lucy discouraged?
   b. Why did her English teacher tell her to do her English composition over?
   c. What had she done with her mistakes?
   d. Why had she used several words incorrectly?
   e. Why hadn't she written her homework on the correct paper?

CHECK-UP

What's the Word?

> 1. give it back
> 2. hand it in
> 3. do it over
> 4. throw it away
> 5. look it up

Listening

Have students complete the exercises as you play the tape or read the following:

Listen and write the missing words.

Dear Alice,

   I'm very discouraged. I'm having a lot of trouble with my girlfriend, and I don't know what to do. The problem is very simple. I'm in love with her, but she isn't in love with me! A few weeks ago, I gave her a ring, but she gave it back. During the past few months I have written several love letters to her, but she has thrown them away. Recently I asked her to marry me. She thought it over for a while, and then she turned me down. Now when I try to call her up she doesn't even want to talk to me. Please help me. I don't know what to do.

"Discouraged Donald"
Denver, Colorado

Answers
1. gave it back
2. thrown them away
3. thought it over
4. turned me down
5. call her up

Text Pages 109–111: *Would You Like to Get Together Today?*

FOCUS

Review of separable two-word verbs and introduction of:

clean up	*figure out*
drop off	*take down*

INTRODUCING THE MODEL

1. Have students look at the model illustration.
2. Set the scene: "Tom is calling his friend Paul."
3. Present the model.
4. Full-Class Choral Repetition.
5. Ask students if they have any questions; check understanding of new vocabulary: *free, drop off, That'll be great, Speak to you then.*

   ### Language Notes

   The expression *Are you free?* means *Are you available?* or *Do you have free time?*

   In *I'd really like to,* the word *I'd* is a contraction of *I would.* The expression *I'd really like to* and similar expressions with *I'd* are often used in polite language for expressing one's wants and needs.

6. Group Choral Repetition.
7. Choral Conversation.
8. Divide the class into pairs and have students practice the model conversation.
9. Call on pairs of students to present the dialog. Have students use their own names in place of *Paul* and *Tom.* If possible, have students hold telephones to add realism as they present the dialog.

   (For additional practice, do Choral Conversation in small groups or by rows.)

SIDE BY SIDE EXERCISES

Examples

1. A. Hi, (_____). This is (_____).
      Would you like to get together today?
   B. I'm afraid I can't. I have to clean up my living room.
   A. Are you free after you clean it up?
   B. I'm afraid not. I also have to throw out all my old newspapers.
   A. Would you like to get together after you throw them out?
   B. I'd really like to, but I can't. I ALSO have to pick up my brother at the train station.
   A. You're really busy today! What do you have to do after you pick him up?
   B. Nothing. But by then I'll probably be EXHAUSTED! Let's get together tomorrow instead.
   A. Fine. I'll call you in the morning.
   B. That'll be great. Speak to you then.

2. A. Hi, (_____). This is (_____). Would you like to get together today?
   B. I'm afraid I can't. I have to clean up my room.
   A. Are you free after you clean it up?
   B. I'm afraid not. I also have to put away my clothes.
   A. Would you like to get together after you put them away?
   B. I'd really like to, but I can't. I ALSO have to do my Algebra homework over.
   A. You're really busy today! What do you have to do after you do it over?
   B. Nothing. But by then I'll probably be EXHAUSTED! Let's get together tomorrow instead.
   A. Fine. I'll call you in the morning.
   B. That'll be great. Speak to you then.

1. **Exercise 1:** Introduce the new expression *clean up*. Call on two students to present the dialog. Then have students practice in pairs.

2. **Exercise 2:** Introduce the new word *Algebra*. Same as above.

3. **Exercises 3–5:**

   > **New vocabulary:** 3. *take down, Christmas decorations, New Year, party decorations, drop off*
   > 4. *figure out, hospital bill, insurance form* 5. *wedding guest, wedding invitation*

   Culture Note

   Exercise 3: Some typical Christmas decorations are a fir tree with colored lights and ornaments (a *Christmas tree*) and a wreath on the front door of one's house.

   Have students practice these exercises in pairs. Then call on one or two pairs to present each exercise.

4. **Exercise 6:** For homework, have students write a new conversation using any two-word verbs they wish. Have students present their dialogs in the next class.

WORKBOOK

Pages 89–91

EXPANSION ACTIVITIES

1. ***What's the Word?***

   a. Write on the board:

call up	hang up	take down
clean up	look up	take off
figure out	pick out	take out
hand in	pick up	think over
	put on	turn off

   > I'll _____.

b. Read the sentences below and have students respond with an appropriate two-word verb from the list on the board. For example:

> Teacher: Your coat is on the floor.
> Student: I'll pick it up.

1. Your coat is on the floor. (pick it up) (hang it up)
2. Which tie should I wear with this suit? (pick it out)
3. We're supposed to write our name, address, and phone number on this form. (fill it out)
4. What does "edible" mean? (look it up)
5. How much is 2436 and 8941? (figure it out)
6. There's a lot of garbage in the kitchen. (take it out)
7. What are you going to do, stay or leave? (think it over)
8. The basement is really dirty! (clean it up)
9. Those pictures on the wall look terrible! (take them down)
10. You should wear those new gloves I gave you. (put them on)
11. That black tie doesn't look very good with your brown suit. (take it off)
12. Who's watching TV? Nobody. (turn it off)
14. I have to talk to you this weekend about something very important. (call you up)

2. *Review of Separable Two-Word Verbs: Why don't you _____ ?*

a. Write on the board:

> A. _____.
> B. Why don't you _____?
>
> A. That's a good idea. I think I'll _____ { him / her / it / them } _____ right now.

b. Write the cues below on word cards.

Divide the class into pairs and give each pair a cue. Have Speaker A start a conversation by reading the cue; then have students continue using the model on the board. For example:

> A. I'd really like to hear some music.
> B. Why don't you turn on the radio?
> A. That's a good idea. I think I'll turn it on right now.

Cues:

1. It's very cold in here.
2. This coat is too warm.
3. My living room is so dirty I can't stand it.
4. I can never remember your phone number.
5. I really don't need these boots during the summer.
6. The birthday party was a week ago. These decorations are starting to look terrible.
7. I'd really like to talk to my friend Jack who lives in New York.
8. I'd really like to know the definition of that word.
9. My homework looks terrible. It has too many mistakes.
10. I really want to wear my blue dress/suit tonight, but it's at the cleaner's.
11. I'd really like to watch the news on TV.
12. I'll never be able to remember the directions to George's house.

Text Page 112: *I Heard from Him Just Last Week*

FOCUS

Introduction of the following inseparable two-word verbs:

call on	*look through*
get along with	*look up to*
get over	*pick on*
hear from	*run into*
	take after

INTRODUCING THE MODEL

1. Have students look at the model illustration.
2. Set the scene: "Two friends are talking. One of them usually gets a letter from his uncle every month."
3. Present the model.
4. Full-Class Choral Repetition.
5. Ask students if they have any questions; check understanding of new vocabulary: *hear from, just last week.*
6. Group Choral Repetition.
7. Choral Conversation.
8. Call on one or two pairs of students to present the dialog.

   (For additional practice, do Choral Conversation in small groups or by rows.)

SIDE BY SIDE EXERCISES

Examples

> 1. A. Have you heard from your cousin Betty recently?
>   B. Yes, I have. As a matter of fact, I heard from her just last week.
>
> 2. A. Have you looked through your old English book recently?
>   B. Yes, I have. As a matter of fact, I looked through it just last week.

1. **Exercise 1:** Call on two students to present the dialog. Then do Choral Repetition and Choral Conversation Practice.
2. **Exercise 2:**

   a. Set the scene: "Some students like to look through their old books. They don't read every word; they just look at their old lessons."

   b. Introduce the new expression *look through*.

   c. Same as above.
3. **Exercises 3–6:**

> **New vocabulary:**   3. *run into*   4. *get over*   5. *call on*   6. *pick on*

Either Full-Class Practice or Pair Practice.

As you introduce each new two-word verb, read the corresponding *set the scene* below.

3. "I haven't seen Mr. Smith in a long time. I usually see him around the school, in the cafeteria, in the library, or in the parking lot."

4. "A friend of mine had the flu recently. She was sick for two days. By the third day she felt better and went back to work."

5. "Some students like it when the teacher asks them questions because they like to talk in front of the class. Others get embarrassed when the teacher asks them questions."

6. "Most sisters and brothers really love each other. But sometimes the older children aren't nice, and they pick on their younger brothers and sisters. Then the younger children cry for 'Mommy' or 'Daddy.' "

HOW ABOUT YOU?

Introduce the new expressions *get along with, take after, look up to*. Write these new expressions on the board; then point to each one as you read the situations below:

"Mary *gets along with* her sister very well. They never argue, and they like each other very much. They enjoy spending time together."

"John *takes after* his father. John's father is good at mathematics. John does very well in math, too. His father can sing very well, and John sings well, too."

"Mr. and Mrs. Smith have a son named Mark. Mark really *looks up to* his parents. He thinks they're wonderful people, and he hopes he'll be like them when he grows up."

Have students answer the questions in pairs or as a class.

WORKBOOK

Page 92

EXPANSION ACTIVITIES

1. *Synonyms: Guess Who!*

   a. Write on the board:

call on	hear from	pick on
get along with	look through	run into
get over	look up to	take after

I don't know. Who _____?

   b. Read the sentences below and have students respond with an appropriate two-word verb from the list on the board. For example:

   Teacher: Guess who I met downtown!
   Student: I don't know. Who did you run into?

   1. Guess who I met downtown! (run into)
   2. Guess who my little brother was fighting with! (pick on)

3. Guess who wrote me a letter! (hear from)
4. Guess which student Mrs. Smith asked about the Civil War! (call on)
5. Guess who I admire! (look up to)
6. Guess which of my parents I'm similar to! (look like)
7. Guess who my favorite friends are! (get along with)
8. Guess who doesn't have the flu anymore! (get over)

2. Create a Story

a. Write on board:

b. Set the scene: "Julie is twelve years old. She's a healthy, happy young girl."

c. Ask the following questions about *Julie*. Have students use their imaginations to make up answers.

1. Julie has two younger brothers. Does she pick on them? (When? Why?)
2. Julie is the best student in her class. Does she get embarrassed when the teacher calls on her?
3. How does she get along with the other students in her class?
4. Julie likes to get letters and phone calls. Who does she like to hear from?
5. Who does Julie look up to? Who looks up to Julie?
6. After school Julie likes to go to the drug store and buy a soda. Who does she hope she runs into there?
7. Last year Julie had a boyfriend, but they broke up. Has she gotten over it yet?

READING: *A Child-Rearing Problem*

FOCUS

Two-word verbs (inseparable)

NEW VOCABULARY

answer (n)	constantly
child rearing (n)	eventually

PREVIEWING THE STORY (optional)

Have students talk about the story title and/or illustration. Introduce new vocabulary.

READING THE STORY

1. Have students read silently, or follow along silently as the story is read aloud by you, by one or more students, or on the tape.
2. Ask students if they have any questions; check understanding of vocabulary.
3. Check students' comprehension, using some or all of the following questions:

   a. How do Timmy and his little sister Patty get along with each other?
   b. What do they constantly do?
   c. When does he pick on her?
   d. When does she pick on him?
   e. Why are their parents concerned?
   f. How have they looked for an answer to their problem?
   g. Have they been successful so far?
   h. What are they hoping?

CHECK-UP

True, False, or Maybe?

1. False
2. True
3. True
4. False
5. Maybe

Choose

1.	a	5.	b
2.	a	6.	b
3.	b	7.	a
4.	b	8.	b

ON YOUR OWN: *May I Help You?*

FOCUS

> Review of separable and inseparable two-word verbs

ON YOUR OWN ACTIVITY

1. Set the scene: "A salesman in a department store is talking to a customer."
2. Go over the conversational model; introduce the new vocabulary.

> **New vocabulary:**
>
> | | | |
> |---|---|---|
> | size | tight | usual |
> | medium | loose | You're in luck. |
> | extra-large | narrow | percent |
> | selection | baggy | regular |
> | try on | No problem at all. | My pleasure. |
> | dressing room | within | |

Language Note

> *May I help you?*, *I think I'll take (it/them)*, *My pleasure*, and *Please come again* are expressions that are typically used in shopping situations.

3. Present Exercise 1 at the bottom of text page 115 with a student. Then do Choral Repetition Practice.
4. Divide the class into pairs; have students practice Exercises 1, 2, and 3.
5. Call on pairs of students to present the exercises.

Example

> 1. A. May I help you?
>   B. Yes, please. I'm looking for a raincoat.
>   A. What size do you wear?
>   B. (Size 40), I think.
>   A. Here. How do you like this one?
>   B. Hmm. I think it's a little too (fancy). Do you have any raincoats that are a little (plainer)?
>   A. Yes. We have a wide selection. Why don't you look through all of our raincoats on your own and pick out the one you like?
>   B. Can I try it on?
>   A. Of course. You can try it on in the dressing room over there.
>
>   (5 minutes later)
>
>   A. Well, how does it fit?
>   B. I'm afraid it's a little too (baggy). Do you have any raincoats that are a little (tighter)?
>   A. Yes, we do. I think you'll like THIS raincoat. It's a little (tighter) than the one you just tried on.

B.   Will you take it back if I decide to return it?

A.   Of course. No problem at all. Just bring it back within (10) days, and we'll give you your money back.

B.   Fine. I think I'll take it. How much does it cost?

A.   The usual price is ($80). But you're in luck! We're having a sale this week, and all of our raincoats are (20) percent off the regular price.

B.   That's a real bargain! I'm glad I decided to buy a raincoat this week. Thanks for your help.

A.   My pleasure. Please come again.

6.   **Exercise 4:**   For homework, have students write a new conversation with any article of clothing they wish. Encourage students to use dictionaries to find new words they wish to use. Have students act out their dialogs in the next class.

WORKBOOK

Page 93

READING: *On Sale*

FOCUS

> Two-word verbs (separable and inseparable)

NEW VOCABULARY

button	go with	plaid
especially	happiness	refund (n)
final	notice	refuse (v)
fit		zipper

PREVIEWING THE STORY (optional)

Have students talk about the story title and/or illustrations. Introduce new vocabulary.

READING THE STORY

1. Have students read silently, or follow along silently as the story is read aloud by you, by one or more students, or on the tape.
2. Ask students if they have any questions; check understanding of vocabulary.
3. Check students' comprehension, using some or all of the following questions:

   a. Why did Melvin go to a men's clothing store yesterday?
   b. What did he look through?
   c. What did he pick out first?
   d. How did it fit?
   e. What did he pick out next?
   f. How did it fit?
   g. Finally, what did he pick out?
   h. How did it fit?
   i. Then what did he decide to buy?
   j. What did he look through?
   k. What did he pick out first?
   l. How did they fit?
   m. What did he pick out next?
   n. How did they fit?
   o. Finally, what did he pick out?
   p. How did they fit?
   q. Why was Melvin especially happy?
   r. Why didn't Melvin's happiness last very long?
   s. What did he do the next day?
   t. Why did the people at the store refuse to give him his money back?
   u. What will Melvin do the next time he buys something on sale?

CHECK-UP

What's the Sequence?

1. Melvin went shopping for clothes yesterday.
2. Melvin picked out a few jackets he really liked.
3. The brown jacket seemed to fit perfectly.
4. He picked out several pairs of trousers.
5. A pair of plaid pants fit very well.
6. He paid only half of the regular price.
7. He walked home feeling very happy.
8. But then, Melvin noticed problems with the jacket and the pants.
9. Melvin went back and asked for a refund.
10. The store refused to give him back his money.
11. He walked home feeling very upset and angry.

Listening

Have students complete the exercises as you play the tape or read the following:

Listen and choose what the people are talking about.

1. A. Have you filled it out yet?
   B. No, I'm having some trouble. Can you help me? (a)

2. A. Where can I try them on?
   B. The dressing room is right over there. (a)

3. A. Now remember, you can't bring them back!
   B. I understand. (a)

4. A. Please drop them off at the school by eight o'clock.
   B. By eight o'clock? Okay. (b)

5. A. Where should I hang them up?
   B. What about over the fireplace? (a)

6. A. Have you thought it over?
   B. Yes, I have. (b)

7. A. It's cold in here.
   B. You're right. I'll turn it on. (b)

8. A. Should we use it up?
   B. No, let's throw it out. (a)

IN YOUR OWN WORDS

1. Make sure students understand the instructions.
2. Have students do the activity as written homework, using a dictionary for any new words they wish to use.
3. Have students present and discuss what they have written, in pairs or as a class.

WORKBOOK ANSWER KEY AND LISTENING SCRIPTS

Page 86 A. WHAT ARE THEY SAYING?

1. pick him up
2. turned it on
3. filled it out
4. hang them up
5. take them back
6. throw them out
7. picked it out
8. put it away
9. call her up

Page 87 B. WHAT ARE THEY SAYING?

1. on
   putting them on
2. in
   hand it in
3. away
   put them away
4. off
   take them off
5. up
   called him up
6. on
   turned it on
7. off
   turn it off
8. back
   bring him back

Page 88 C. WHAT ARE THEY SAYING?

1. turned it off
2. think it over
3. look it up
4. turn it/him down
5. gave them back
6. written it down
7. do it over
8. used it up
9. cross them out
10. threw it away

Page 89 D. GETTING READY FOR A VACATION

1. drop off
2. take out
3. figure out
4. put away
5. throw out, pick up
6. take down
7. pick out
8. give back
9. call up

Page 90 E. HOW ABOUT YOU?

1. hand in
2. clean up
3. pick up
4. write down
5. turn on
6. . . . .

Page 90 F. WHAT SHOULD THEY DO?

1. turn it off
2. look it up
3. call him up
4. write it down
5. put them away
6. think it over
7. do it over
8. take them down
9. pick her up
10. give it back
11. Put it on
12. throw them out
13. use it up

Page 92 G. COME UP WITH THE RIGHT ANSWER

1. take after
   take after her
2. got over it
3. called on me

4. ran into
   ran into him
5. get along with
   get along with her
6. heard from
   hear from him
7. pick on me
8. looking through
   looked through them
9. look up to
   look up to me

Page 93 H. LISTEN

Listen to each sentence. Put a circle around the appropriate answer.

1. What's the price of this shirt?
2. This jacket fits you.
3. All of the clothes in this store are 20 percent off this week.
4. How many pairs of shoes did you try on?
5. Yesterday, while I was in the post office, I ran into my old math teacher.
6. Please turn on the air conditioner.

7. Peter takes after his mother.
8. I really look up to my father.
9. My sister picks on me all the time.
10. Did you throw away our last can of paint?
11. I've just gotten over the flu.
12. Why did you turn him down?
13. Have you heard from Betty?
14. George picked out a new suit for his wedding today.
15. David dropped his sister off at the dentist's office.
16. I'm going to pick Jack up at the airport.
17. Joe left the air conditioner on in his apartment all day while he was at work.
18. Mary doesn't get along with her brother.

Answers

1.	b	10.	c
2.	a	11.	b
3.	a	12.	c
4.	b	13.	b
5.	b	14.	c
6.	a	15.	a
7.	b	16.	b
8.	c	17.	c
9.	b	18.	a

GRAMMAR

Connectors
Too/So

I'm hungry.	I am, too. So am I.
I can swim.	I can, too. So can I.
I've seen that movie.	I have, too. So have I.
I have a car.	I do, too. So do I.
I worked yesterday.	I did, too. So did I.

Either/Neither

I'm not hungry.	I'm not either. Neither am I.
I can't swim.	I can't either. Neither can I.
I haven't seen that movie.	I haven't either. Neither have I.
I don't have a car.	I don't either. Neither do I.
I didn't work.	I didn't either. Neither did I.

But

I don't sing, **but** my sister does.

I'm tired,	and he is, too. and so is he.
He'll be busy,	and she will, too. and so will she.
She's been sick,	and he has, too. and so has he.
They sing,	and she does, too. and so does she.
She studied,	and I did, too. and so did I.

I'm not tired,	and he isn't either. and neither is he.
He won't be busy,	and she won't either. and neither will she.
She hasn't been sick,	and he hasn't either. and neither has he.
They don't sing,	and she doesn't either. and neither does she.
She didn't study,	and I didn't either. and neither did I.

FUNCTIONS

Asking for and Reporting Information

Do you know *the answer to question number 9*?

How do you know *Mr. and Mrs. Jenkins*?

Have you heard *tomorrow's weather forecast*?

Where were you when *the accident happened*?
I was *standing on the corner*.

Tell me about your *skills*.
Tell me about your *educational background*.
Have you had *any special vocational training*?
When can you *start*?

Expressing Likes

I like *strawberry ice cream*.

I appreciate *literature, music, and other beautiful things*.

He enjoys *sports*.

Expressing Dislikes

I don't like *war movies*.
I don't like *fairy tales* very much.

Inquiring about Want-Desire

Why do *you and your husband* want to *enroll in my dance class*?

What *do you and Fred* want to *talk to me about*?

Why don't *you and your friends* want to *come to the ballgame*?

Expressing Want-Desire

He wants *this parking space*.

She doesn't want to *take the garbage out*.

Inquiring about Ability

Can you *baby-sit for us tomorrow night*?

Expressing Ability

I can *speak four languages fluently*.

Expressing Inability

I'm not a very good *tennis player*.

I can't *dance the cha cha*.
I can't *sing* very well.

I won't be able to *go bowling next Monday night*.

Inquiring about Intention

What *are you and your girlfriend* going to do *tomorrow*?

Expressing Intention

I'm going to *study at the library*.

Extending an Invitation

Are you interested in *seeing a movie tonight*?
Do you want to *go dancing tonight*?

Describing

My brother and I are exactly the same.
My brother and I are very different.

I'm *tall and thin*.
I have *brown eyes and black curly hair*.
He's very *outgoing and popular*.

Inquiring about Feelings-Emotions

Why do *you and your sister* look so frightened?

Why were *you and your wife* so nervous?

Alphabetical List

actor (100)
actress (101)
airport (211)
angry (84)
apples (175)

backache (143)
baker (99)
bakery (69)
bananas (174)
bank (10)
barber shop (70)
basement (6)
bathroom (2)
beans (181)
beauty parlor (71)
bedroom (1)
beer (190)
big (49)
blush (93)
bowl (129)
bread (179)
brush _____ teeth (41, 151)
bus driver (104)
businesswoman (115)
businessman (114)
bus station (64)
butcher shop (203)
butter (192)

cafeteria (68)
candy store (212)
carpenter (108)
celery (197)
cheap (50)
cheese (176)
chef (98)
church (60)
clean (159)
clean _____ apartment (36)
clean _____ yard (35)
clinic (72)
cloudy (52)
coffee (199)
cold [adjective] (80)
cold [ailment] (146)
cold [weather] (58)
computer programmer (118)
concert hall (220)
cook (19, 148)
cookies (185)
cool (57)
courthouse (219)
crackers (180)
cry (86, 160)

dance (28, 125, 152)
dancer (97)
dentist (107)
department store (73)
dining room (4)

doctor (105)
doctor's office (74)
do _____ exercises (38)
drink (27, 170)
drug store (67)

earache (144)
eat (21, 168)
eggs (173)
embarrassed (85)
expensive (50)

factory worker (113)
feed _____ dog (34)
fire station (62)
fix _____ car (31, 150)
fix _____ sink (32)
fix _____ TV (33)
flour (184)

garage (8)
garlic (182)
gas station (66)
get up (135)
go bowling (129)
go dancing (125)
go jogging (131)
go sailing (130)
go shopping (128)
go skating (126)
go skiing (127)
go swimming (124)
go to a baseball game (122)
go to a movie (121)
go to the bank (133)
go to the doctor (132)

handsome (47)
happy (77)
hardware store (214)
have lunch/dinner (123)
headache (140)
heavy (44)
high school (205)
hospital (17)
hot [adjective] (81)
hot [weather] (55)
hotel (208)
hungry (82)

ice cream (178)

jam and jelly (189)
jog (131)

kitchen (5)

large (49)
laundromat (65)
lettuce (195)
library (12)

listen to the radio (30, 161)
little (49)
living room (3)

mailman (119)
mayonnaise (191)
mechanic (94)
melon (194)
milk (177)
motel (216)
movie theater (14)
museum (207)

nervous (75)
new (45)
newsstand (213)
nurse (106)

old (43, 45)
onions (202)
orange juice (188)

paint (37, 164)
painter (120)
park (13)
parking lot (210)
pears (196)
pepper (200)
perspire (91)
pet shop (215)
plant flowers (166)
play baseball (26)
play cards (25, 155)
playground (209)
play the piano (24)
plumber (109)
policeman (111)
police station (61)
poor (48)
post office (15)
pretty (46)
put on clothes (138)

raining (53)
read (18)
rest (167)
restaurant (9)
rice (183)
rich (48)

sad (76)
sail (130)
salesman (116)
saleswoman (117)
salt (200)
school (59)
scientist (110)
secretary (112)
shave (157)
shiver (90)
shoe store (204)

shop (128)
shopping mall (217)
short (42)
shout (88, 163)
sick (79)
sing (29, 169)
singer (96)
sit (171)
skate (126)
ski (127)
sleep (23)
small (49)
smile (87, 158)
smoke (89, 153)
snowing (54)
soda (187)
sore throat (145)
stomachache (141)
study (20, 156)
sugar (198)
sunny (51)
supermarket (11)
swim (124)

take a bath (136)
take a shower (137)
talk on the telephone (149)
tall (42)
tea (201)
teacher (102)
thin (44)
thirsty (83)
tired (78)
tomatoes (172)
toothache (142)
train station (63)
truck driver (103)
TV station (218)

ugly (46, 47)
university (206)

violinist (95)
visit a friend in the
  hospital (134)

wait for the bus (165)
warm (56)
wash _____ car (39)
wash _____ clothes (40)
watch TV (22, 154)
wine (193)
work (147)
write (139)

yard (7)
yawn (92, 162)
yogurt (186)
young (43)

zoo (16)

263

Categories

Adjectives

angry (84)
big (49)
cheap (50)
cold (80)
embarrassed (85)
expensive (50)
handsome (47)
happy (77)
heavy (44)
hot (81)
hungry (82)
large (49)
little (49)
nervous (75)
new (45)
old (43, 45)
poor (48)
pretty (46)
sad (76)
short (42)
sick (79)
small (49)
tall (42)
thin (44)
thirsty (83)
tired (78)
rich (48)
ugly (46, 47)
young (43)

Ailments

backache (143)
cold (146)
earache (144)
headache (140)
sore throat (145)
stomachache (141)
toothache (142)

Foods

apples (175)
bananas (174)
beans (181)
beer (190)
bread (179)
butter (192)
celery (197)
cheese (176)
coffee (199)
cookies (185)
crackers (180)
eggs (173)
flour (184)
garlic (182)
ice cream (178)
jam and jelly (189)
lettuce (195)
mayonnaise (191)
melon (194)
milk (177)
onions (202)
orange juice (188)
pears (196)
pepper (200)
rice (183)
soda (187)
sugar (198)
tea (201)
tomatoes (172)
wine (193)
yogurt (180)

Community

airport (211)
bakery (69)
bank (10)
barber shop (70)
beauty parlor (71)
bus station (64)
butcher shop (203)
cafeteria (68)
candy store (212)
church (60)
clinic (72)
concert hall (220)
courthouse (219)
department store (73)
doctor's office (74)
drug store (67)
fire station (62)
gas station (66)
hardware store (214)
high school (205)
hospital (17)
hotel (208)
laundromat (65)
library (12)
motel (216)
movie theater (14)
museum (207)
newsstand (213)
park (13)
parking lot (210)
pet shop (215)
playground (209)
police station (61)
post office (15)
restaurant (9)
school (59)
shopping mall (217)
supermarket (11)
train station (63)
TV station (218)
university (206)
zoo (16)

Home

basement (6)
bathroom (2)
bedroom (1)
dining room (4)
garage (8)
kitchen (5)
living room (3)
yard (7)

Professions

actor (100)
actress (101)
baker (99)
bus driver (104)
businessman (114)
businesswoman (115)
carpenter (108)
chef (98)
computer programmer (118)
dancer (97)
dentist (107)
doctor (105)
factory worker (113)
mailman (119)
mechanic (94)
nurse (106)
painter (120)
plumber (109)
policeman (111)
salesman (116)
saleswoman (117)
scientist (110)
secretary (112)
singer (96)
teacher (102)
truck driver (103)
violinist (95)

Verbs

blush (93)
bowl (129)
brush _____ teeth (41, 151)
clean (159)
clean _____ apartment (36)
clean _____ yard (35)
cook (19, 148)
cry (86, 160)
dance (28, 125, 152)
do _____ exercises (38)
drink (27, 170)
eat (21, 168)
feed _____ dog (34)
fix _____ car (31, 150)
fix _____ sink (32)
fix _____ TV (33)
get up (135)
go bowling (129)
go dancing (125)
go jogging (131)
go sailing (130)
go shopping (128)
go skating (126)
go skiing (127)
go swimming (124)
go to a baseball game (122)
go to a movie (121)
go to the bank (133)
go to the doctor (132)
have lunch/dinner (123)
jog (131)
listen to the radio (30, 161)
paint (37, 164)
perspire (91)
plant flowers (166)
play baseball (26)
play cards (25, 155)
play the piano (24)
put on clothes (138)
read (18)
rest (167)
sail (130)
shave (157)
shiver (90)
shop (128)
shout (88, 163)
sing (29, 169)
sit (171)
skate (126)
ski (127)
sleep (23)
smile (87, 158)
smoke (89, 153)
study (20, 156)
swim (124)
take a bath (136)
take a shower (137)
talk on the telephone (149)
visit a friend in the hospital (134)
wait for the bus (165)
wash _____ car (39)
wash _____ clothes (40)
watch TV (22, 154)
work (147)
write (139)
yawn (92, 162)

Weather

cloudy (52)
cold (58)
cool (57)
hot (55)
raining (53)
snowing (54)
sunny (51)
warm (56)